Faith, Family, Friends and Farm

Henry

Thank you for your efforts on behalf
of the St Mary's Medical Center Foundation.

We believe that honoring the Past
and the lessons it provides is often one
of the best ways to ensure a
brighter Future.

Andy   Mike

Faith, Family Friends and Farm

STORIES OF AND FROM HERITAGE FARM MUSEUM & VILLAGE

By Mike & Audy Perry

www.heritagefarmmuseum.com

CONTENTS

FOREWORD
BY AUDY PERRY

Over the past 40 years, I have heard my dad give hundreds of speeches. As a lawyer; banker; deacon; community leader; college president; Fortune 500 Company board member; hall of famer for two universities, a law school, a city and the WV Chamber of Commerce; WV Banker of the Decade; Humanitarian Award recipient; and Parent; there have been many opportunities to hear my dad speak. After one such occasion, wherein Dad was introducing the late, great Senator Robert C. Byrd to a standing-room-only crowd at Marshall University, one of my law partners quipped "I love your Dad's speeches – he always hits the 4Fs." I asked him what he meant and he said that Dad always hits the Four "F"s – Faith, Family, Friends and Farm. What a wonderful description of his life.

Although there have been many speeches, there were few written accounts of his words. Until now. The purpose of this book is to share Dad's story of Faith, Family, Friends and Farm in his own words. What you are about to read is a collection of writings taken from Dad's own "legal pad" letters, handwritten thoughts on how he fell in love with his God, his wife, his farm and the people of Appalachia. Along the way, I have included a few of my own observations about the 4Fs to confirm to him that I have been listening. I hope you enjoy our walk together as we stroll to, through and beyond a very special place known to us as Heritage Farm.

INTRODUCTION
BY MIKE PERRY

A friend once told me that if you were raised on a farm, you worked yourself to death as an adult in order to never have to live on a farm again. But if you were *not* raised on a farm, he said, you worked yourself to death in order to someday be able to live on a farm.

I do not know how accurate that is – my wife, Henriella, and I were not raised on a farm, nor were our parents – but in 1973 we did move with our three children, ages 12, 10 and 2, from a beautiful brick home in Huntington, West Virginia, to a burnt log cabin on a 150-acre farm. A smooth-talking salesman would have called it a "fixer upper." It had no indoor plumbing, no central heat or air conditioning and only one strand of electricity with two plugs (one for a light and the other for a radio). And did I mention burnt? The cabin was so badly burnt, in fact, that the entire roof, consisting of wood shingles covered with tin, had to be replaced. The logs were covered with cardboard and paper, which had to be removed along with years of accumulated dirt, nests and other disgusting things. And, because of the terms in the selling of a home in the city, we had only 90 days to make that cabin livable.

Thanks to friends, we were able (just barely) to get in within that three-month period. We installed indoor plumbing, but our well water smelled like rotten eggs. We heated with wood that we burned in a cast iron stove in the living room. I spent every evening cutting, splitting and carrying firewood. My wife spent a considerable portion of her day putting wood in the stove and trying to keep the house warm.

Comfortable? It would be a number of years before we could honestly say we were comfortable. Still, there was very little complaining. Every day was a new adventure. Our lives were filled with challenges, but also with a reasonable chance of overcoming them.

And in the final analysis, that just may be a great definition of happiness.

We believed that raising children on a farm would provide wonderful opportunities for them to learn lessons about life and to develop their character and abilities better than in similar opportunities in the city. Friends were skeptical, to say the least. Moving to the farm meant much more than simply changing school districts. In many ways, we would be completely altering our daily routines.

Now 38 years later, our children are adults, married, with children of their own, eight, in fact -- our wonderful grandchildren. People often ask if we ever regretted our decision to change our lives so dramatically. The answer is absolutely not. This book will show you why we think our move to the farm was one of the best decisions we ever made.

As we worked to make our new farm home livable, we fell in love with our Appalachian ancestors, those men and women who came over the mountains into

2

what is now West Virginia, Eastern Kentucky and Southern Ohio. We imagined them clearing the land, building their homes, raising their own food and making their own clothes from materials they processed themselves. Our ancestors' hard work and perseverance have given to us a quality of life that, unfortunately, many of us take for granted today.

As a tribute to these remarkable people, our family developed Heritage Farm Museum & Village. More than two dozen log buildings and other structures now stand around our original cabin, facilities we built from the materials we salvaged from original log cabins and barns found throughout West Virginia, Kentucky and Ohio. Six museums, five log homes, a log church, blacksmith shop, one-room school and several meeting facilities now stand around our first farm home. In them, we exhibit thousands of artifacts, tools and implements used by our Appalachian forebears. We show not only how the tools were used, but also how those tools evolved through the creativity and inventiveness of these people. A big part of the story we have to tell is their efforts to make their lives better and more productive, raising more food and manufacturing more products than anyone could have ever imagined.

The Perry children all love animals and have developed a respect for life and, sadly, an understanding of its frailties. On the farm, they learned many lessons of life and death, joy and sorrow, pride and disappointment as they took responsibility for their animals and realized the creatures' dependency upon them. They learned that love includes making sacrifices, being faithful and diligent. Sure, I suppose these lessons also could have been learned with pets in the city. However, feeding, watering, grooming, exercising and caring for horses and other large animals on the farm gave our children a perspective they probably would not have found with city cats, dogs and goldfish. Cleaning out stalls and shoveling manure builds more than just muscles.

All of us – the children and their parents alike – learned from a life on the farm. We discovered the old-fashioned way where food comes from and how hard it is to prepare the ground, plant, hoe, harvest and then preserve our food. We butchered hogs, picked fruit and berries and stirred apple butter after peeling what seemed like thousands of apples. We learned how much better everything tasted fresh from our own garden compared to the same items bought from a grocery store. We built and repaired fences and raised livestock. We experienced the joys and the sorrows of calving. We often ponder how the "Facts of Life" our children learned came from observing the mating of animals and the genetics of breeding, including the adverse consequences of selecting poor stock. (That background, we've always believed, must explain their excellent selection of intelligent and talented spouses for themselves and the fabulous children they have raised.) Meanwhile, day in and day out, the children learned the powerful lessons of human dependence on the weather - - the importance of sun and rain in the right amounts and at the right time. Of course, the farm's most important lesson was our ultimate dependency on our Heavenly Father to provide for us.

And today, even though the kids are grown now, the farm's gifts haven't stopped coming.

These days Henriella and I are constantly reminded of another great benefit to our move to the farm: the

4

many visitors to our museums, particularly the thousands of school children. Dreams do come true, they learn here, if you team up those dreams with the same hard work and determination that our ancestors had years ago when they first cleared the land and began settling their farms. We tell them: Look at our beautiful "Old Log Cabin" now after many years of blood, sweat and tears. Dreams do still come true. That continues to be a main reason we created Heritage Farm Museum & Village -- to make sure the children are encouraged to dream big dreams for themselves and to realize what it takes to make those dreams come true.

Moving ourselves and the children to the farm proved to be an even wiser decision than we could have ever imagined. Yes, it entailed a lot of hard work and a lot of sacrifices. There were plenty of highs and lows, laughing and crying and peace and pain. But isn't that what life is all about, regardless of where you live? So in answer to our skeptical friends from long ago, no, we have never regretted our decision to come to the country.

This book tells the story of Heritage Farm, how it came to be and what we have learned from our years here. In the next section -- "A Love Story" -- we tell how the farm grew from a simple weekend retreat into a living legacy and tribute to the creative minds and spirits of our Appalachian ancestors. In the second section – "Lessons from the Barnyard" -- our son, Audy Perry creates a series of suitable-for-Sunday-school stories built on what he has learned from decades of loving and caring for the farm's animals. In the final section -- "Reflections" -- I share what I have discovered from years of research and contemplation of history as

Henriella and I created the buildings that are today's Heritage Farm Museum & Village.

We believe that wherever you live, you would do well to slow down and spend time at places like Heritage Farm. Come and be reminded of how fortunate we all are to live in this country and be blessed by the lessons and values that have been passed down from generation to generation. Studying the past is the best way to insure a great future. That's why the motto of Heritage Farm Museum & Village has always been: "Experience the Past (Yesteryear) to gain an Appreciation for the Present (Today) and Dream of a brighter Future (Tomorrow)."

A LOVE STORY
BY MIKE PERRY

I

We are often asked about the beginning of Heritage Farm Museum & Village. How and when did it start, certainly, but more often, *why* did it start?

I would love to be able to tell you it was in response to a childhood dream or that it was part of a well-organized plan to accomplish some long-standing purpose. How wonderful and poetic it would be if my wife, Henriella, and I were preserving an ancestral home established many generations ago by one of our own ancestors, perhaps someone who was a great general or a hero who had won many great battles. How exciting if we were restoring ancient agricultural implements, steam tractors, buggies, wagons and early automobiles and trucks that were actually used by our own forefathers. How fantastic to read their diaries and journals describing their lives. How appropriate it would be if we had been trained and educated historians or, better still, gifted mechanics, carpenters, or at least possessed with "jack of all trades" skills. And while we're dreaming, wouldn't it be wonderful if the land had produced great mineral wealth or if our ancestors had left us with a large inheritance in order to preserve our rich heritage and educate future generations about it?

That wouldn't be true, though, and truth is the only foundation worth building on, even if it is not very glamorous.

The reality is Henriella and I never lived on a farm. Neither did our parents. She and I were raised in Huntington, West Virginia, by honest, God-fearing, hard-working parents who loved us and our siblings. They sacrificed a great deal to make sure we got a good education, which they believed would be our passports to good things they dreamed of for their children.

We were fortunate. Like millions across this great nation in the 1940s and '50s, our parents were wonderful people who went to work and did their best to make ends meet, often under difficult circumstances. They were from humble backgrounds. Our fathers graduated from high school and started to work in a local factory. Later, they left the factory and worked for themselves. Our mothers were both very devoted to their children. (Henriella's mother, Virginia Mylar, at 99, is still devoted to us all, still going strong.) Although neither of our mothers had much of a formal education, each greatly influenced our values and helped mold us into the adults we are today. Their stories are our story and the story of so many parents like them. They are the average people who made this a great country, and their hard work, beliefs and sacrifices should never be forgotten.

The story of Heritage Farm Museum & Village really begins with our effort to pay tribute to our parents and the countless number of people like them down through American history. Not generals and heroes, in the traditional sense, but real heroes in *our* minds, because day in and day out, they did their best without complaining to raise families with a hope of a better future for them. They were builders, dreamers, doers. We owe them a debt of gratitude that can never be paid.

Many great monuments and museums appropriately celebrate specific individuals and major events in history. However, Heritage Farm Museum & Village's focus is on untold stories of people who never enjoyed 15 minutes of fame and never read about themselves in the newspapers, people who quietly got the job done. These were the workers without whom the great capitalists and industrialists would never have been able to build this great country.

It is also the story of the great inventors and the creative geniuses who took their ideas and brought them to life, but from a different perspective than perhaps you are accustomed to. Everyone loves to tell the story of Henry Ford and his Model T and how it changed the world. But at Heritage Farm Museum & Village, we're even more interested in the story of the hundreds of thousands of people who left Europe and Asia and so many other places to cross dangerous oceans to come to America, the land of opportunity. Ours is also the story of later generations who would venture out in another way, leaving the security of their farms, families and friends to work in factories in cities such as Detroit, Chicago and Pittsburgh. Instead of living in the beauty of the country, with its greenery and spaciousness, they learned to live on the third floor of a large building in a small apartment. The mothers gave up the comfort of living near their relatives and friends to establish a home in these new surroundings. The children no longer went to a rural one-room school where everyone knew each other but now were in large schools with a great diversity of cultures and races. The fathers, who had left working in the fields and the satisfaction of raising the food to provide for their families, found themselves punching in and out on time clocks -- new machines which seemed to question their word and integrity. They performed mind-numbing, repetitive work, like putting the right front headlight on each automobile chassis as it passed by in a constant parade, hour after hour, day after day, week after week and month after month.

Talk about change and enduring change! These people could teach us a lot about how we, not only as individuals and families, but also as companies, organizations and even governments, need to deal with the dramatic medical, scientific, cultural and technological changes often engulfing us today. They endured change and so can we, with the same attitude and determination.

All of us prefer the familiar ways we have always done things, like the way an old shoe fits. However, history – especially the history of the average man and woman – shows us we must be careful that our reluctance does not cause us to become so opposed to change that we fail to look and accept new and better ways of doing things.

Change is what Heritage Farm Museum & Village is all about. We tell the story of the average American, first as a settler, then a farmer, then a craftsman or a factory worker. Our topic is how the major inventions – the reaper, steam engine, electricity and the automobile –

changed his life and the vital role this average man played in this remarkable story.

But I am getting ahead of myself. We need to come back to history a little closer to home and see how two kids who grew up in a small city became involved in something as important to them as Heritage Farm Museum & Village.

First and foremost, Heritage Farm Museum & Village is a love story, the tale of:

– A boy and a girl who meet as children.

– A man who gives up golf because his wife lovingly asks him to find something they could do together as a family.

– A woman who gives up a beautiful brick home in the city and moves to a log cabin in the country because of her love for her husband and family.

It is also the story of a couple's love for family and heritage and their passion to share that heritage with others.

The story begins in fifth grade when a small boy arrived at a new school and is dazzled by a petite, beautiful girl just his size, a girl with twinkling eyes and long brown hair. He would soon tell his mother that he was going to marry that girl some day. Years later, his mother would remember that story to tell when the boy and girl were married.

But an interlude of six years would teach the boy some valuable lessons. For instance, there was the one he learned during the school's sixth grade train trip to Washington, D.C., when this little girl and two other tall, attractive girls all sent the young boy notes asking him whom he loved best. He thought he was being clever when he wrote back to *each* of them proclaiming he loved her the best. The result was three lessons at once -- wisdom that would stay with him the rest of his life.

(1) Do not put it in writing.

(2) Girls talk.

(3) Monogamy is a prudent course.

He immediately went from three girlfriends to none!

It was six years later, in their senior year of high school, that the school choir director, Mrs. Heinz, and her substitute, Janice Chandler, now Janice Gold, played cupid, deciding the boy and girl should sing a love duet "My Hero" at the school's graduation program. The teachers insisted that the couple practice frequently and to hold hands while projecting the emotions of the song.

Their matchmaking worked. Soon after, the pair began dating, which lasted through four years of college. Mike Perry and Henriella Mylar were married upon his graduation from Marshall College, now Marshall University. After marriage, the newlyweds moved to Morgantown, West Virginia, where he graduated three years later from the West Virginia University College of Law. In 1961, the Perrys returned to Huntington where Mike began practicing with a distinguished law firm. Their daughter, Michele Marie, was born the same year followed by another daughter, Melanie Lynn, in 1964 and a son, Audy Michael Perry, Jr., in 1971.

II

In the early days of our marriage, I was working long hours at the office. Any free time I had I spent playing golf. One day Henriella very sweetly and lovingly suggested that, rather than my being away with work or golf, it would be wonderful if she and I could do something together with the children on Saturdays. Maybe it was how she said it. Or maybe it was my frustration at not getting any better at golf.

In any event, we launched something new and started going antiquing every Saturday with the children. As our budget we established the amount that I was spending playing golf, which was about $5 a week in green fees. Initially in our scavenging, we collected kitchen devices, meat grinders and small hand tools. Gradually we started thinking bigger, expanding into collecting old wooden washing machines, scrub boards and related items.

Now, more than 30 years later, what you see at Heritage Farm Museum & Village is the product of all those Saturdays. Our museums are filled with various treasures we found as we regularly raised our antiquing budget to reflect our increased earnings as a lawyer and then as a banker. (Confession: Once bitten by the antique bug, we rationalized my "golf budget" by imagining that we were spending money that we otherwise would have laid out for golf trips to, say, Hilton Head and Scotland. It was a feeble but earnest effort to justify what had become a very important part of our lives.)

The growing Perry family moved several times, but by 1973, we were finally living in our dream house: a large brick home on the south side of town with a lovely corner lot near public schools where our children could walk to excellent schools from the first grade through senior high. Meanwhile, we also had begun spending every spare moment on a 200-acre farm that my father, Austin Lee Perry, had purchased shortly before his untimely death at the age of 52. He bought the property from the heirs of a gentleman named Colonel Cornelius Blatt.

After my father's death, this farm, tucked in the rolling hills near the west end of the city, became a refuge and haven for my mother and our family. With

help from my Uncle Zora, my father's oldest brother, and his wife, Aunt Toy, we began working to make the farmhouse livable for our joint weekend use. While structurally sound, the farmhouse had no indoor plumbing and almost no electricity. In deplorable shape, it was surrounded by overgrown trees and shrubs. Even today, the house holds tremendous memories for Henriella and me. In the wake of my father's death, this was, of course, a time of healing for us. Then with my mother's death, the house again underwent considerable modernization and became a new home for our daughter, Melanie, who had married

Mark Hall. They occupied the house with their two children until they bought a beautiful farm of their own in Spring Valley.

Today a major part of Heritage Farm Museum & Village – all the buildings north of the entrance, including all the structures in the village proper – sits on this original Blatt property. The old farmhouse became our Hollyberry Inn, one of five bed and breakfasts inns we rent throughout the year. Meanwhile, all the buildings south of the entrance, including the School, original barn and our home, are a part of what used to be called the Schafer Farm. How we came to acquire this farm is a big part of our story.

Bill and Andrew Schafer were brothers who lived on the adjoining land south of the Blatt farm. The Schafers and the Blatts were part of a group of Germans who settled in our part of West Virginia in the late 1800s in an area now known as German Ridge. Most were dairy farmers who later operated wagon and truck farms selling milk, cheeses and other produce to the residents of nearby Huntington.

Henriella and I learned much over the years from the Schafer brothers, who were very much a part of the Huntington area. In fact, after moving here as young children with their parents, they never traveled more than twenty miles from home except for Bill's deployment to France in World War I. It was fascinating to hear how the world had changed during their lifetimes, and their stories have become part of our own, even part of our family lore and traditions. We still smile, for instance, when we recall the day Henriella and I were visiting with them and their phone rang. Bill, the younger brother, answered it, and after a very brief conversation, hung up the phone. Then after a moment, Bill proudly proclaimed to us that while he could "make'm" and "take'm," his brother, Andrew, could only "take'm." Our clueless expressions must have shown him that his pride was completely lost on us, so Bill explained: He could call other people on the phone, while brother Andrew could only answer the phone. It turned out that Bill had learned the numbers of two of his German neighbors whom he could call when he needed something. He was pleased with himself, having a considerable skill that his older brother did not possess. Though I found the story hilarious at the time, I now often recall it as I struggled to learn to use my computer. For a while, I could "take" e-mails but couldn't "make'm," which my young grandchildren thought was very funny since they themselves, of course, could "make'm" and "take'm."

After Andrew's death, Bill moved to a nursing home and the Schafers decided to sell the home place. Henriella and I wanted to buy it. Their old barn interested us, but moreover, the property included a large piece of flat bottomland that connected with my mother's place, the former Blatt farm. However, the prospects did not look good. The price exceeded what we felt comfortable paying for a weekend retreat. Also, other potential buyers were sniffing around, including one who wanted to develop the land into a trailer park.

One day, Henriella asked how negotiations were going. I told her I had given up. It was just too expensive. And that's when she said the thing that changed our lives.

Had I thought, she asked, about selling our house in the city and moving to the farm?

Well, yes, I *had* thought about that. Often. But I couldn't ask her and the children to make such a move. The old log house on the property, partially burned, needed lots of work. It had no indoor plumbing and only one light and one plug for a radio. Most of all, if we sold our house in the city to buy this property, we would have no extra money to remodel or even,

hopefully, build a new more modern home.

"Let's do it," she said.

I quickly agreed. I believe neither of us wanted to take time to over-think this decision.

It is a good thing I was a lawyer. After agreeing on the purchase price, I had to find 64 people spread out across the United States to get their signatures on the deed. Bill and Andrew had a number of brothers and a sister, all of whom had died before them.

Once that was done, all we had to do was to sell our house. We did this in the spring of 1973, but that led to the next challenge. Our buyers needed to take possession within 90 days so their children could start school in their new neighborhood. That deadline gave the Perry family only three months to make a new life in an old farmhouse.

III

Everything needed painting. In fact, it was in such disrepair that at one point I asked Bill Schafer just when the old place had last seen a paint brush.

Right after the war, he said.

Uh, *which* war, I said.

Why, World War I, he said.

It had not been painted in more than 50 years, and a recent fire had destroyed the roof, damaging some of the logs.

Henriella and I never worked so hard in our lives. But with the help of family and friends -- particularly my brother, Rory Perry, my brother-in-law, Bill Chambers, and my dear friend, Lawrence Pauley, who was my building and construction mentor -- we made the house livable and moved in within 90 days. After working in my office and all day most Saturdays, we put in a septic tank, an indoor bathroom, running water in the kitchen and more adequate electrical service. We replaced the tin roof and removed the wood shake shingles underneath which had burnt. Our water came from a well and had too much iron and sulfur and smelled like rotten eggs. We had no central heat or air conditioning. We heated the house with a cast iron stove in the living room with wood we split and carried in throughout the day. It heated us as we cut it, split it, carried it and finally as we burnt it. Talk about staying in shape! Our fitness program didn't require going to the "Y" to work out. And note I say *we* because my wife and I and our children all were involved in all aspects of the work, both the doing and the cleaning up afterwards. And cleaning up was a formidable challenge, because some of the logs had been burnt while the other log walls had been covered with paper, cardboard and boards in an effort to keep bugs out and heat in (with obvious poor results in both campaigns). It took many years and much hard work and sacrifice with no vacations and not much free time for recreation or entertainment.

Many people, including some of my law partners, wondered if we had lost our minds, gone broke or both. At times, we were not sure ourselves.

But we did know that we enjoyed the country and we thought that once we got past the initial difficulties, it would be a wonderful place to raise a family. The children would have horses and other animals and so many opportunities to learn responsibility and to strengthen their character.

Of course, those "initial difficulties" meant all our spare time and all our spare money would be committed to making the house habitable. Actually, we at first didn't intend to stay in the old log house for long. On the contrary, we envisioned building a grand new house across the road in a beautiful field with plenty of wide-open space.

But something happened as we worked on the old place. Over time, we started examining the logs of our house. Each log, we noticed, was different than all the others, with various notches and cuts. Only later would we learn the unique marks were made by axes and adzes wielded by men many years ago. We fell in love. There's no other way to put it. We fell in love, not only with our house, but also with the people who built it. And not just the people who built *our* house but hundreds and thousands just like them who built other log cabins and houses.

Countless times over the years since then, we have been asked why we left the comfort and convenience of the city to move to the country, a place many of our friends thought to be lonely and desolate. It was not unlike how we ourselves wondered why the Schafers and the earlier settlers moved into this area and built this house and the many others like it in the Appalachian region of southwest West Virginia, eastern Kentucky and southeastern Ohio. How did they survive? How did they cope without all the modern conveniences that we take for granted? How did they deal with all the changes going on around them as new inventions drastically changed everything? How did these people earn their living? What did it mean to go from the agriculture age (when at one time 97 percent of the people were involved in producing food) to today, when less than 3 percent of the people are involved in agriculture? What was it like for Bill and Andrew Schafer and countless others like them to go in onelife time from traveling to town in a horse-drawn wagon to riding a steam train or driving a Model T Ford? How did it feel for them to suddenly be watching planes flying overhead? Or to read about a fellow West Virginian, General Chuck Yeager, flying faster than the speed of sound? Or hear on the radio (as they did not own a television) about men landing on the moon?

History was coming alive for us in that old log cabin! Not just the history we learned in school, the dry recitation of dates of when things were invented and when wars were fought. The history around us was the story of how average people, living where we lived, coped with change, monumental change, perhaps more change than anybody had ever experienced before in one lifetime.

And moving into the house was only the start of the adventure, not the ending. The more we read and studied about our Appalachian ancestors, the more we wanted to experience firsthand many of the things they did. We wanted to raise much of our own food in a garden, can and preserve food, plant corn fields, pick nuts, fruits and berries, raise and butcher our own meat, churn butter, make lye soap, build fences, clear brush and trees, cut hay and store it in the barn, put chopped silage in the silo, milk a cow, feed the chickens and gather the eggs. Honestly, some of these things we did only once in the years to come, like butchering a hog. It did not take us long to be thankful that we did not have to do *that* to survive. And putting up hay – it was hard work, often done in extremely hot weather.

And to learn, we were fortunate to have as our neighbors those children and grandchildren of the original German people who settled here in the late 1800s, friends who were gracious in teaching us how to do the things they themselves had learned from their parents and grandparents. Sure, in the beginning they were a little suspicious of us, the first non-Germans to occupy any of the land inhabited by their ancestors. Initially, they also were concerned we were going to subdivide the land and sell it off in lots. But once they quit laughing at the "city slickers" who were practically helpless in their eyes, they became wonderful neighbors, generous and hospitable. It always amazed us how they could figure out how to move extremely heavy objects and do other complex things that I am not sure some of my contractor and engineering friends could have done. Compared to them, I, with my 19 years of education, was often embarrassed by what I did not know. Humbling.

Of course, all of this was not some sudden inspiration. It was a gradual development over a few years, as we worked first on the log house, then on the log barn, then on other buildings. We've always been sorry we did not find any of the personal effects or farm implements of the Schafers, and since neither of us had inherited such from our own ancestors, we were somewhat ignorant of that part of history. (Fortunately in September 2006 we were able to purchase the Schafers' original 1927 Farmall Tractor from their nephew, Raymond Beiter, and it now is a proud addition to our collection at the museum.) However, stashed throughout the house and in every nook and cranny we could find was the accumulated "junk," as we called the treasures from our countless Saturdays of antiquing.

And we had Henriella, who was constantly keeping the project on track. I've always been in awe of the pioneer woman, the glue who held those early families together. Now, the more we continued on our own adventure, I realized that Henriella, my beautiful wife for more than 50 years, would have made a marvelous pioneer. She has all the various skills, talents and characteristics of our Appalachian ancestors: industrious, creative, resourceful, determined, compassionate and – perhaps most important – an adventuresome spirit. Henriella did all of this while cooking three meals a day, caring for and transporting the children, washing and ironing, sewing curtains and clothes, teaching the girls to do the same, painting and wallpapering, feeding wood into the stove in the winter, caring for the many animals on the farm – dogs, cats, pigs, sheep, chickens, goats – providing first aid and medical treatment for everyone, never having time to get sick herself, playing and teaching the children to play the piano, spending time with her husband and never letting him feel neglected or not special and unloved, being active in her church and women's prayer and study groups and even trying to teach herself to play the fiddle. And through it all, there was always patience and a true sense of inner peace. Satisfaction was hers at the end of the day, because she had done her best, and she enjoyed a good night's sleep with a clear conscious awaking to a new day in the morning ready to go again.

After being there only a short time, Henriella and I began calling our home "Heritage Farm," and for the next half dozen years, we would work on expanding our own living space. We connected the original log house with the nearby smokehouse, which became our bedroom. We made the connecting space into a family room. In the 1980s, we started converting the old dairy barn where our girls had kept horses on the ground floor and our son and I had played basketball in what had previously been a hayloft. And all the while, the family continued the Saturday outings to collect "the Old Stuff."

IV

Our first museum grew out of a simple need just to get that ever-growing collection of Old Stuff out of the house and out of every other building in which we had stored it. In what we now realize was the next defining moment in the story of Heritage Farm Museum & Village, we started converting the barn as an exhibition area for our collection.

With it we also had a new approach in mind. We wanted the exhibition area to tell a story, something different from the majority of the museums we had visited on our rare family vacations. Most museums are excellent at depicting a particular time in history. One might focus on pre-1840 or post-1860 and assure that everything displayed is authentic to that period, down to the varieties of grass, fruit and animals. We applaud that, but we had something else in mind. We wanted our museum to demonstrate progress. The inventiveness of man was our chief interest, and how imagination and experimentation changed everything, particularly in rural Appalachia. Across the country, you can visit many large, splendid houses and farms of famous and prosperous people and you can learn a lot of history in your travels. When you come to see us, you'll get a different perspective: the homes, farms and lives of average people, people who often struggled just to survive. Ours would be the story of a remarkable people – our Appalachian ancestors – and the consequences of their fighting (or even worse, of their sometimes ignoring) change.

In that converted barn our new work began. We started humbly, by displaying our collection of 100 washing machines, many of them constructed with wood. The machines range from those of the 1870s to the fancier ones of the 1920s. Washing machines might seem like an odd starting point. Actually, though, these machines beautifully demonstrate the ingenuity and creativity of men and the companies they formed to build and sell these inventions. Not only that, they also illustrate change in one of the hardest, most time-consuming jobs in the lives of women and how "keeping up with the Jones" (and the American free enterprise system) gradually provided us with a quality of life we take for granted today with our modern laundry facilities.

As the exhibition grew, we also wanted to demonstrate the many skills that the early pioneer homesteader needed. These rugged settlers needed to learn how to put a roof over the heads of their families, how to put food in their stomachs and clothes on their bodies. We especially wanted to illustrate how life was different on this side of the Appalachian Mountains. On the eastern side of the mountains, there were primarily communities, villages and towns. But on the western slopes, there were hardy individuals who had to be able to make everything that they couldn't bring with them from back east. Rugged, brave, resilient and creative, these hard-working men and women endured unimaginable challenges and difficulties. For instance, in the East, if someone needed a wool coat, he purchased the wool and had it combed, dyed, spun, woven and tailored. The whole process could involve five or six different craftsmen. But on the other side of the mountains, all these tasks had to be done by the one family, at least until more new neighbors arrived to share their skills and knowledge.

Nowadays on tours at Heritage Farm Museum & Village, we explain these differences by showing how logs and stone were cut and shaped, how gardens were plowed and how food was cooked and preserved. But almost any of the tools and practices of the settlers can illustrate this point, from the churns, spinning wheels and looms to the tools of the shoemakers, coopers and carpenters. We can even show our guests what everyday life was like without modern doctors and dentists by showing what those early offices looked like when they finally moved into the communities.

All this was done in what used to be a simple barn. We redid the floors, beams and walls – essentially everything! In the end, our home, Heritage Farm, now became Heritage Farm Museum.

But it has never been a *farm museum*. That is to say, it is not a collection of horse-drawn implements rotting in an old farmhouse, barn and outbuildings. It is not a collection of old stuff piled in a warehouse for people to wander around reading about ancient devices used in various and sundry manners. It is not a monument to our countless hours and dollars spent over many years as collectors and antique buffs. (People still confuse us because of our name. In retrospect, perhaps it would have been wiser for us to have called it The Museum at Heritage Farm.)

Meanwhile, the work we did on the barn after finishing our house in the 1980s inspired us to continue. Just like the creative pioneers we continued to learn about, we now had new ideas of our own. Next we began work to create our Country Store, renovating the shed where the Schafers had kept their tractors and related farming equipment, all of which had been removed by their heirs.

And as we worked, we researched -- reading, studying and talking to old-timers. And much of the results of these decades of research we share in the third section of this book, "Reflections."

All during this time we continued to collect logs, stones and chimneys from within 50 miles in West Virginia, Kentucky and Ohio. We built the Strawberry Inn, now one of our bed and breakfast inns. All three of our children, as adults, have lived there at one time or another. We tried to build our cabins in such a manner that people could experience what it was like to have lived in the 1800s but with all the modern 21st century conveniences, except TVs.

With the Country Store and our first inn, we were growing beyond our initial museum to create a *village*.

V

We started construction of the village in the 1990s, building on a large cornfield on the original Blatt farm that my brother and I had inherited two decades earlier. (I had previously bought his share of the farm.) In other words, none of the buildings you see today at Heritage Farm Museum & Village were located on the farm. In fact, except for the one-room schoolhouse and three walls of the church, nothing existed anywhere as you now see them. It would not have been a very effective cornfield to have had a village in the middle of it!

To build our village, we began over a number of years disassembling more than 50 log buildings, most of them from long-unoccupied log cabins. Unfortunately, many of them had been vacant for so many years that they were starting to deteriorate. In addition, many had gone through modernization or had seen additions built on, so for our purposes, it often required multiple buildings to complete one structurally sound log cabin or other building in the village. We also decided to add modern conveniences – bathrooms, kitchens, laundry rooms and closets – so it was not unusual to take as many as five or six buildings to complete each inn.

Some visitors ask why we did not restore the cabins to their original conditions in the 1800s, without water, electricity or heating and air-conditioning. To answer, we harken back to those inspirational early settlers who have taught us much about how to survive. Just as our ancestors' goal was to create a self-sustaining farm and community, we wanted Heritage Farm Museum & Village to support itself. It quickly became clear to us that providing tours primarily to school children was not going to provide enough funding to support the museum. Something more had to be done to establish a firm financial footing for the future. We considered many options. Perhaps we could give the museum to the state, the city or Marshall University? However, none of these possibilities promised the resources needed to maintain the museum and village. Besides, like most communities, ours already had too many organizations desperate for limited funds.

So we struck out in a different direction. As we developed the village, we also created facilities we could rent out for multiple purposes and use for educational purposes. Quickly we discovered that people wanted to spend time in the 1800s, but *not without* their 21st century conveniences. For that reason, we created our bed and breakfast facilities – the Applebutter Inn, the Strawberry Inn, the Blackberry Inn, the Hollyberry Inn and now the Woodbury Inn – where a family or grandparents with their grandchildren could stay overnight, surrounded by antique furnishings with a rustic ambiance but without giving up their creature comforts.

And we added the log Welcome Center, used today for dinners, receptions, parties and reunions because it can seat up to 90 people. Like much of the village, the Welcome Center is new, but also old. It is constructed of logs from six different cabins, one of which was one of the earliest dwellings in Westmoreland in Wayne County, West Virginia. Later we added the more modern Heritage Hall for the same purposes but with seating for 200 people. It even has enough space for a large square dance and community sing. Today all of these facilities are used for weddings, family and school reunions, various church events and other meetings and activities.

Meanwhile, for those wanting a more authentic 19th century experience, we are completing the Kress Conway Homestead Cabin. Unlike our bed and breakfast inns, it will have no modern conveniences inside. It will be furnished with rope beds and other antique furnishings of the period before electricity. This cabin, relocated from German Ridge area near us, originally was occupied by the Kress family, one of our first settlers. The cabin was given to us by the Kress grandson, Jerry Conway. One of the most important buildings at the museum, the cabin will give people a better appreciation of what it was like to be a homesteader living alone without the support of a town or village or even many neighbors.

Of course, farms are as much about animals as they are about people. Our children have always loved animals, from their earlier days growing up on this land, and that love has inspired our Farm Zoo. The special bond between animals and people is part of our heritage, when these animals were not just pets but were essential to the survival of the early settlers and homesteaders. Dogs, cats, sheep, goats, cows and horses all had jobs to do.

The major educational buildings in the village are designed to be more accessible and convenient than the Barn Museum, which has multiple stairs:

-- The Progress Museum shows how life evolved as major inventions were developed. Kitchens of 1850, 1900 and 1925 are featured in this building, as well as large model railroad layouts of various scales, printing, weaving and more.

-- The Transportation Museum shows the evolution of travel from horse-drawn vehicles like the Conestoga wagon and a Wells Fargo stagecoach, to a 1908 electric truck, a 1910 Sears automobile and a 1915 Model T along with tools needed to build and repair the cars and trucks. There also is a large model demonstrating the importance of steam in changing our world.

-- The Industry Museum explores the importance of the agricultural, timber, coal, gas and glass industries in Appalachia. It contains a small exhibition coal mine that you can walk through. It also contains an example of an early machine shop and a blacksmith shop powered by belt-driven machinery. In addition to these museums, the Village also contains the Children's Hands-On Activity Center, the Heritage Museum, a neighborhood Country Store, Blacksmith Shop, a Broom Maker's Shop, a Gristmill, a Sawmill and a Shingle Mill.

One of the most popular buildings in the village is our marvelous Log Church, complete with a bell in its tower that has been joyously rung as a part of every wedding celebrated here on our grounds. Churches often served as a school and town hall before other separate buildings could be constructed. It was the backbone of the community and today symbolizes our forefathers' strong faith in God. We are so pleased that so many young couples want to start their lives together by coming here to exchange vows.

Throughout the village, beautiful quilts and coverlets in the various buildings (particularly in the "Green Room" of Heritage Hall) capture the essence of the people we honor. Beautiful and intricate stitching did not make our ancestors one degree warmer, but work embodied the resourcefulness, skill, artistry, imagination, determination and pride of the people. Oh, the stories they could tell! These same characteristics are preserved in the handwork of the men who made chairs, other furniture and tools, often at night in front of the fireplace while the wife quilted. We only wish our collection could come alive to tell us the stories of these extraordinary people.

VI

The greatest quarterback needs a strong line to protect him and give him time to throw. He also needs a talented, capable end who can evade his challengers and catch the ball. They all require each other to be successful as a team. They also need gifted coaches, not only to develop the players' diverse skills, but also to motivate them, molding them into a cohesive group. Often the most important job for the coach is reminding the team members that they need each other, helping each manage egos and images of self-importance.

So it is with life, at home, work or play. Successes throughout history reflect times when people working together accomplish great things. An excellent example that we show in our museums is the story of the railroad and its impact on our lives and country. Railroads required not only many talented inventors to *create* but also other inventors to *improve* the machines, locomotives, cars and rails. It also required capitalists, bankers and investors who would risk their money to make these things happen. And it required coal miners, timber men and countless others to provide the fuel to run these machines and to make the steel. Coal and timber had been in West Virginia forever, but there was little demand for it until the building of the railroad and the need to produce steel and steam. That is the story of West Virginia and our move from the Agricultural Age to the Industrial Age.

Coal and timber were removed from the hills by thousands of workers because thousands of workers had built the railroad tracks, tunnels and trestles through, under and between the West Virginia mountains to get the coal and timber to thousands of workers who made the locomotives, rails and countless other steel products needed for a growing nation. These thousands of workers would not have had jobs without the capital invested in these enterprises and the managerial skills needed to coordinate many complex tasks. Of course, sometimes these industrialists forgot that they could not accomplish anything without the hard work, imagination, creativity and bravery of the workers. And sometimes the workers forgot the importance of capital and leadership. Times were very difficult for all when each forgot the other. Our history is *their* history – both the times when they remembered to work together and when they forgot to do so – and the resulting victories and difficulties that ensued in bloody battles are our legacy.

Today we still need inventors and discoverers dreaming up new ideas, products and services. We still need investors, money and bankers to help make those dreams into realities. We still need an educated, trained, productive work force, though today they compete in a global market, not merely the local and regional markets of the past. And today the competition is not management or the shareholders, but the other companies often in distant parts of the world working hard to put them out of business. Just as a team needs a good coach, we need honest, competent management to coordinate and motivate us, and governments to support us in our global efforts, people who understand how to create an environment in which businesses and their productive workers can prosper.

Too often we forget what it took for us to have today's quality of life. Worse than that, we take it for granted. But if we study the *past*, we gain an appreciation of the *present* and can plan and dream about a wonderful *future*, for not only ourselves, but also for those who follow us.

At Heritage Farm Museum & Village, we showcase inventors and companies that changed the world, but we also emphasize the worker and his skills and determination, without which none of this would have occurred. We hope you leave us with a renewed appreciation of our ancestors and their efforts to make a better place for us. We also hope you have a better understanding of the consequences if the present generation does not work together for the future of their children and grandchildren.

Will it be our legacy to be the first generation *not* to have left the world a better place to live, work and play? I don't think so. Our study of history teaches us that the good old days weren't so good, but the *people* certainly were. If we approach the uncertainties of the future with the same firm confidence they had, we will succeed as they did. It is hard to imagine what exciting new ideas will arise in the next 25 years, what new power sources, means of communication and transportation and medical advances. Progress *is* exciting. You must just embrace change and never yield to the disastrous temptation to fight it or, worse still, ignore it.

Come and see us. Spend an hour, a day or a week. Leave with a new sense of history, an appreciation of how fortunate we are to be living today, and an excitement about the future!

VII

From time to time we have wondered whether we had lost our minds by devoting so much time and money to Heritage Farm Museum and Village. As a banker I certainly learned better than to invest in something that required considerable upkeep and maintenance and produced very little income, but Henriella and I have always concluded that we were doing what we were supposed to do. God and the people of our church have always been a very important part of our life, and it seemed to us that every time we struggled with our doubts or with the need for more money, God provided. Equally important, if not more so, each time we needed help and expertise to understand a new effort, God provided such people often out of nowhere. Some would call this luck, but we have always seen it as God's providence and blessing.

Henriella and I certainly did not have all the skills necessary to produce what we today call Heritage Farm Museum & Village. We have been blessed to meet and work with a wonderful group of people who have made our dream a reality. We met great people who taught us the beauty and skills of the early craftsmen as they lovingly restored and brought back to life many of our Saturday treasures. We met many others who have the considerable carpentry, construction and other skills to salvage old logs and stone and help create the many buildings and facilities we enjoy today. Truly, without them, it could not have happened, and we thank God for them. I am reminded of the creative geniuses who restored the 1908 electric truck, the miniature amusement park, the Sawmill, the blacksmith shop and the Machine Shop, among other things. They give us confidence that the ingenuity and creativity of our ancestors is still alive and well today.

We also appreciate the dedication, commitment, skill and faithfulness of our guides who are absolutely essential to the museum and its future. We request that our guests visit the museum with a knowledgeable guide who doesn't merely recite what things are, but more importantly, tries to tell the stories of our ancestors. Without these guides, it might become just a display of "old stuff," which would represent a terrible loss. They truly make a difference in what we are trying to establish and leave as a legacy.

I could go on and should, but won't. Something of the magnitude of Heritage Farm Museum and Village just doesn't happen, and to these people and to the hundreds of volunteers and friends, who over the years have helped make it possible, we say, "Thank you and God Bless!"

LESSONS FROM THE BARNYARD
BY AUDY PERRY

Animals have been an integral part of my life for almost four decades. Growing up on the farm, I was the youngest member of our family, and I always loved playing with the dogs, cats, ducks, cows and anything else we could find roaming the hills and splashing in the creeks. When our family farm became Heritage Farm Museum & Village, the new petting zoo was a great

opportunity for me to share my love of animals with children of all ages.

God could have created a world of just plants and humans to tell His story, but I believe He provided the gift of animals to teach us about ourselves and our relationship to an almighty, yet loving, God.

This section of our book contains some of my favorite animal insights over the years. I almost subtitled it "Four weaks to a new ewe." Although I enjoyed the pun, I didn't wish to profess to be any kind of "Seven steps to Jesus" story. God is so much bigger than a method or formula. However, I do invite you to a curious journey through the barnyard. You can obviously read this entire section in one setting but if you enjoyed your first pass through, I recommend that you go back and read just one story each day for four weeks. Each week focuses on a different "weak" area of our lives that limits our ability to fully enjoy a relationship with the Creator of the universe.

Take a look at God through a different set of eyes each day and along the way you may discover a *new you* as you learn about a *new ewe,* the one and only Lamb of God.

Weak #1 -- DISCONTENTMENT

The first lie man fell for – all the way back in the book of Genesis – was the thought that there was something better "over there" and that God was really holding out on us, failing to be content with God's provision and boundaries.

1. Have you ever purred in God's lap?

The cat is the only animal I know that has an auditory, physical response to contentment: the purr. It is gratifying not only to the feline but also the owner.

The other morning, I sat down in the zoo during feeding time, and Charky and Pipa (9-month-old kitties that I rescued from the pound) jumped up on my lap, got comfy and immediately began to purr. They were safe in the lap of their master.

Like Charky and Pipa, each day we have a choice. We can choose to chase sparkly objects or little pieces of string, which is fun for a while but soon becomes tiresome and pointless. Or we can choose to be contented in the lap of our Master. What will you choose today?

Keep your lives free from the love of money and be content with what you have, because God has said, "Never will I leave you; never will I forsake you." Hebrews 13:5

2. Walking the fence line

If you have ever released cows into a new pasture, the result is always the same. They munch on the new delicacies for a while and then it begins: a steady march to explore the fence line. No matter how large the pasture, the cows set out to walk the boundaries of their enclosure. And if a fence is down or there is a gap, you can be sure that is the first place they will discover!

We humans are no different. Something about limits hurts our pride. Why can't I go there/why can't I do that? But like the good farmer, God has placed those boundaries for our protection. He knows what lurks beyond the fence line that will lead to our distress and destruction.

Then the man and his wife heard the sound of the LORD God as he was walking in the garden in the cool of the day, and they hid from the LORD God among the trees of the garden. Genesis 3:8

3. Why does other people's stuff look better?

Carrie was a large brown goat who loved having children scratch behind her long floppy ears and pet her smooth coat. She was a joy, but there was one thing that Carrie loved more than attention. Food. She would get into all kinds of messes trying to get to other animals' food (and her belly was ample evidence that she was not in any way missing a meal). One day she went too far. I came for the morning feeding and found her dead, hanging almost 12 inches off the ground with her head stuck between two logs. She had gone to great lengths to try to taste the llama's hay from the adjoining enclosure. The really troubling part was that her own hay bin was full *of the very same hay* but she lost her life because someone else's looked like more fun/better. How often are we like Carrie, going to great lengths to obtain the things that other people have, when all the while we already have all we need?

"You shall not covet your neighbor's house. You shall not covet your neighbor's wife, or his male or female servant, his ox or donkey, or anything that belongs to your neighbor." Exodus 20:17

4. Buckethead

We have fed our lamb, Mary, pretty much at the same time every morning and each day of her long life. Every morning she gets her hay. Every morning she gets her grain. Every morning. Every morning. So I must say it was a little disappointing to find Mary with the neighboring llama's feed bucket stuck on her head one morning. Apparently Mary thought we would fail (for the first time) to  supply her needs. Instead of relying on the steady provisions of her Master, she wanted some extra and was willing to explore what others may have received. What a pitiful sight, white wool fleece capped by a big black bucket emanating a panicked and echoing BAAAAAA!

How often are we like Mary? Our Master has never failed to provide for our needs, and yet we want to take matters into our own hands and see what we can gain for ourselves – and end up being embarrassed bucketheads waiting for the Master to come set us free from our own folly.

"Therefore I tell you, do not worry about your life, what you will eat or drink; or about your body, what you will wear. Is not life more than food, and the body more than clothes? Look at the birds of the air; they do not sow or reap or store away in barns,

and yet your heavenly Father feeds them. Are you not much more valuable than they? Can any one of you by worrying add a single hour to your life?" Matthew 6:25-27

5. Defeated

Have you ever worked really hard at something, planned it all out, worked out all the details (you think), and then have it be a total failure? I have. One time I

ordered a dozen prairie dogs because I thought the kids would enjoy watching them dig their tunnels, scurry around for food and let out their cute little barks. I studied up on them and every source spoke of their great digging prowess, so we dug down deep, laying barriers under the ground and then loaded the piles of dirt on top. We used small wire mesh on the sides so people could not accidentally get bitten or scratched, and we placed mesh netting over the top of the large enclosure so hawks could not swoop down and take the little guys away.

Delivery Day -- so excited, so prepared, so defeated. After discovering that their tunnels couldn't go any deeper, the prairie dogs began scaling right up the wire sides, chewing through the mesh netting up top and flinging themselves off the sides of the enclosure, then running in all directions.

Life challenges are like that sometimes -- we spend so much of our time and energy on one aspect of a known weakness that we get completely blindsided by the bigger picture. I was so focused on preventing "the dig" that I didn't even consider the possibility of "the climb." How about you? Are you so focused on one of your weaknesses that you are unwittingly creating a bigger problem? Seek the Creator's wisdom to fully contemplate your situation so that you may be mature and complete.

Let perseverance finish its work so that you may be mature and complete, not lacking anything. If any of you lacks wisdom, you should ask God, who gives generously to all without finding fault, and it will be given to you. James 1:4-5

6. Beyond words

Have you ever seen God use one part of His creation to speak to another? Maddie was a beautiful, spirited paint who was well trained but liked to always test the boundaries with myself and her other handlers. Tiffany was a young woman whose love for horses transcended her deaf ears and muted mouth. When Tiffany first came to our farm, I had difficulty understanding anything she was trying to communicate,

but Maddie knew exactly what Tiffany wanted: a ride. It was amazing. In the presence of Tiffany, that spirited mare immediately quieted down and lowered  her head for the bridle and from step one, they were in sync, turning left, going faster, up the hill, turning right, down the hill, slowing then stopping back where they had begun. The look on Tiffany's face was priceless: sheer joy.

God is ever present and can use anything and everything to accomplish His purposes. That day, I witnessed the Creator using one part of His creation to show love to another of His beloved creations.

For you created my inmost being; you knit me together in my mother's womb. I praise you because I am fearfully and wonderfully made; your works are wonderful, I know that full well. My frame was not hidden from you when I was made in the secret place, when I was woven together in the depths of the earth. Your eyes saw my unformed body; all the days ordained for me were written in your book before one of them came to be. Psalm 139:13-16

7. A mystery

There is something mysterious about a horse. Why does this great creature of power and intelligence lower itself to the desires of man? I am reminded of Psalm 8:4

 relative to God and man: "What is man that you are mindful of him." In God's response to Job, this mystery is given as evidence of God's dominion. Job is asked, "Do you give the horse his strength or clothe his neck with a flowing mane. ... He paws

fiercely, rejoicing in his strength . He laughs at fear, afraid of nothing. ... He cannot stand still when the trumpet sounds."

At your next opportunity, take a galloping ride on a horse and experience one of God's intimate gifts to mankind. Riding a speeding horse is like encountering God, sometimes frightening, sometimes painful, but oh so exhilarating and satisfying.

"Do you give the horse its strength or clothe its neck with a flowing mane? Do you make it leap like a locust, striking terror with its proud snorting? It paws fiercely, rejoicing in its strength, and charges into the fray. It laughs at fear, afraid of nothing; it does not shy away from the sword. The quiver rattles against its side, along with the flashing spear and lance. In frenzied excitement it eats up the ground; it cannot stand still when the trumpet sounds. Job 39:19-24

Weak #2 -- ME FIRST

The second weakness of man came soon after the first when Cain failed to contain his jealous disappointment for not having finished first. This insatiable appetite to be considered better than others is often the cause for many ruined lives.

8. All this over 47 cents worth of dog food

At 1:15 a.m. on a Sunday morning, I was awakened by the barking of my agitated dogs. I opened my back door and find it was pouring rain and my dogs had

caught a thief red-handed. Yes, a raccoon had invaded their feed bin and they were voicing their disapproval. Not wanting to get wet, I reached for an old baseball and threw it at the bandit. With uncharacteristic accuracy, I hit it in the side. Proud of myself, I was certain the raccoon would run away and I could go back to sleep. No such luck. Instead, the raccoon proceeded to scale the corner of my house and onto the roof.

A $100 repair bill and a very scary attic meeting later, the raccoon was no longer living at my house. However, then it dawned on me. I lost a night's sleep and $100 in the defense of about 47 cents worth of dog food! If I had just let the dogs into the garage, it would have been much easier, safer and less costly.

Many battles in our life are like that. We go into situations thinking the only way to *win* is to defeat everyone who opposes us. We expend massive amounts of time, energy and resources fighting battles that could be avoided altogether if we would just pause and look for alternative solutions that don't escalate the situation.

But the wisdom that comes from heaven is first of all pure; then peace-loving, considerate, submissive, full of mercy and good fruit, impartial and sincere. Peacemakers who sow in peace reap a harvest of righteousness. James 3:17,18

9. Maddie and Tom

One of the funniest sights I got to enjoy over and over again was feeding time in the northern pasture. The pasture was home to two wonderful creatures -- a beautiful, powerful horse named Maddie and a turkey named Tom who had eaten so many of Maddie's leftovers that he now was too fat to fly.

Each day, I would drive past them at the front gate and I would stop my truck at the far end to fill the feed bins. Then it would come, a flat-out race of two very different competitors. The contest would pit Maddie's powerful gallop and flowing mane and Tom's awkward waddle and gangly feathers sticking out all over. One beautiful and graceful, the other goofy and disheveled, they both ran toward their Master for his attention and provision.

It gives me great comfort to know that I can love them both because I imagine God looking out at all his varied flock, taking joy not only in those that are beautiful, but also in those of us who waddle.

"The LORD does not look at the things people look at. People look at the outward appearance, but the LORD looks at the heart." I Samuel 16:7b

10. Ernie

Over the years we have had many types of animals, all with their own unique attitudes and behaviors. Often we put different animals together to teach them that they

can all get along, cats with rabbits, ducks with chickens, llamas with horses, donkeys with dogs, cows with pigs. This integration especially helps with the petting zoo. If a rabbit can put up with the antics of a cat, then a few minutes with a 4-year-old human isn't much of a challenge.

Of all our "can't we all just get along" creatures, none were better at it than Ernie, our rhea, which is South America's version of an ostrich. Over his long life, Ernie shared living space with donkeys, llamas, goats, sheep, rabbits, ducks, chickens, peacocks, cats and his longtime favorite, geese. Remarkably, Ernie could get along with anybody. His secret was humbleness and patience. Even though he was faster than most, taller than many and capable of a wicked kick with his foot or strike with his beak, he held those attributes in reserve. Peace, he seemed to know, was easier if a new pasture mate had time to build some confidence by showing off its own special talents for everybody in the new location.

It is a good lesson to remember. We all want to be impressive, but when we try to impress ourselves *upon* another without understanding his or her own abilities and strengths, the result usually isn't respect and mutual benefit, but jealousy, envy, anger and resentment.

Be completely humble and gentle; be patient, bearing with one another in love. Ephesians 4:2

11. Run, Bucky, run

When my oldest daughter was about 3 years old, we had brother/sister puppies named Buck and Morgan. They were great dogs and minded, usually. But they could not be restrained from playing in the road and chasing cars, despite our sternly disciplining them for such dangerous behavior. Sadly, my daughter saw it the day that Morgan ran out into

the road and was hit and killed by a big, brown UPS delivery truck.

For months thereafter, anytime my daughter saw a big, brown UPS truck, she would scream "Run, Bucky, Run." It was her passionate plea to make sure her remaining dog avoided the danger. My little girl couldn't comprehend all of life's intricate options and consequences, but she clearly saw this one: that Bucky could end up like Morgan if he got near that big thing.

Are we as alert and helpful to our friends? When we see danger for our friends in the choices they are making, do we passionately warn them? Do we help them resist and flee?

Remember this: Whoever turns a sinner from the error of their way will save them from death and cover over a multitude of sins. James 5:20

12. Not in my car

Bo had broken the rules again. He had wandered off and was up to no good down the road when I got  the call from a neighbor. It was raining. Bo was dirty. And the only vehicle I had available to go chase my dog was my nice, new clean car. When he spotted me, Bo came running. I began cheerfully calling his name, hoping he would follow me back home without me or my car getting filthy. And the plan was working! Bo was following my car back home. But then he saw the several deer running up on the hill, and in a flash, he had taken off full speed, no longer interested in following me. Because I hadn't wanted to get dirty, I had no way of helping him avoid his temptation to run away.

So it is sometimes with our Christian brothers and sisters struggling with sin. We know they are headed for trouble and we want to help, so we cheerfully call their name and hope they will simply follow us home. However, when their next round of temptation hits, we lose them because we weren't willing to "allow a little dirt in our car."

To the weak I became weak, to win the weak. I have become all things to all people so that by all possible means I might save some. I Corinthians 9:22

13. Scout

Let's take another look at my earlier story about the prairie dogs (Story #5) and this time, instead of focusing on defeated me, let's focus on the victorious

prairie dogs. Their victory is quite remarkable. When confronted with a new situation where all they had previously known led to dead-ends, they adopted a completely new tactic and succeeded. For their entire lives on the flat, dusty prairie, digging had always worked. Digging had enabled them to escape predators and weather, find food and more. But now suddenly digging *wasn't* working in this new situation.

Scout was the first of my prairie dogs to try something new. He put his made-for-digging claws into the wire mesh on the side of the enclosure and began slowly pulling himself up. When he reached the top, he let out a sentinel bark and all the other prairie dogs quickly followed. Having witnessed Scout's success, the other prairie dogs scaled the sides much quicker because they now knew it could be done. Scout's new way of thinking for the use of his talents was a "lid lifter" to his entire community.

What might you "Scout out" today? Perhaps God is calling you to take a fresh look at using your talents for a greater good.

So it is with you. Since you are eager for gifts of the Spirit, try to excel in those that build up the church. I Corinthians 14:12

14. Pecking order

It never fails. Put a group of any animals together and immediately they all begin jockeying for position. Everyone must know – or be shown – their rank in the new hierarchy. Feathers fly, fur is mauled, things are scratched and no one gets any rest until one emerges as superior to another, right down the line to the lowest in the group. Left to our own instincts, humans are no different -- scratching, clawing and back biting until everyone  knows where we stand. Someone must be lower on the totem pole.

This is so different from the Kingdom of Heaven, where Jesus says we should love our neighbor as our self and that the first shall be last. There is authority and order in His Kingdom but it is based upon love and sacrifice, not force and bragging.

Jesus called them together and said, "You know that the rulers of the Gentiles lord it over them, and their high officials exercise authority over them. Not so with you. Instead, whoever wants to become great among you must be your servant, and whoever wants to be first must be your slave -- just as the Son of Man did not come to be served, but to serve, and to give his life as a ransom for many." Matthew 20:25-28

Weak #3 – DISOBEDIENCE

Genesis Chapter 6 explains that before long mankind was so disobedient and morally bankrupt that God chose to start all over -- and the animals would also suffer for our disobedience.

15. That is not the response he was expecting!

I got a new dog from the pound. He was a beautiful black lab mix who wanted nothing more than to please his new master and show him how worthy he was of being saved from the pound (or at least, to be good enough so that someone never again would say, "I don't want you anymore").

He tried so hard, but his problem was he didn't know the rules. All he had were his instincts. One day he killed one of my chickens – and couldn't have been prouder! He thought for sure that when I saw his accomplishment, he was going to receive a big reward. Boy, was he surprised!

This reminded me of Apostle Paul who, in his Saul days, thought for sure he was pleasing God by killing the Christians. Boy, was *he* surprised when God showed up! We all sometimes carelessly run only on instincts and don't really understand what actually pleases the Master: obedience.

[Jesus replied] "You are my friends if you do what I command." John 15:14

16. More to the story

Adopting a grown dog from the pound is quite an experience. As he tries to learn how to live well in his new home, he makes many mistakes, some of them repeatedly!

For our new black lab, when he realized that he was in trouble, I tried to teach him that he didn't have to run away, that this was not a "one and done" existence. Perhaps his earlier life was not met with much grace, but I wanted him to learn that his new master chose him  specifically for rescue and loved him enough to teach him how to live well in his new environment.

God chose each one of us specifically for rescue. He knows it will take time for us to learn from the Master how to live well and learn of his love and compassion for our lives. Don't run away.

The thief comes only to steal and kill and destroy; I have come that they may have life, and have it to the full. John 10:10

17. Escape artist

Cuddles was a black pound puppy (primarily Chow) whose job was to protect the other animals in the

pasture. She usually did a good job, but also would take any opportunity to create a gap, hole or low fence that she could use to run free. Maybe it doesn't seem like such a big deal, because she was always waiting at the gate the next morning to be put back into the pasture. She would even proudly show me where she had escaped!

The problem was not that she was letting me down on the protection of the other animals. The problem was that her escapes were endangering herself. Cuddles had a good bark and in the pitch black from a distance, it could be imposing enough to convince the prowling coyotes and wild dogs to just move on. However, when she was out among them, these rogues discovered she was just a little thing, weighing no more than 20 pounds. Her bark was considerably bigger than her bite!

Like Cuddles, we sometimes think it harmless and exciting to escape from our Godly duties of always doing the right thing. It seems fun and even our *right* to break out for a little while and be wild. We fully intend to return to the fold in the morning. We can even repent and confess by revealing the weak spot from which we escaped. But, of course, the real danger is that when we are outside of the protective boundaries God has provided, our destruction isn't always immediate. However, it is imminent and eventually the Master comes one morning to find only a mangled mess laying at the gate wishing it had never left the pasture.

For lack of discipline they will die, led astray by their own great folly. Proverbs 5:23

18. Invisible fence

When I failed at training my full grown, adopted, pound dog to stay inside the boundaries of our farm, I resorted to installing an "invisible fence." This is a technology that applies a mild correction to his collar

when he goes too far. After we installed it, my daughter was watching me train the dog to respect his boundaries.

"That's great," she said. "God should install invisible fences for us to keep us out of trouble and danger."

I laughed. "Yeah," I said, "that would make it a lot easier, wouldn't it?"

Only later did it hit me (my own little shock collar) that God has given us Christians the gift of the Holy Spirit, to live inside of us to help guide us in making the right decisions. The Holy Spirit provides that *mental correction* when we are straying beyond our proper boundaries. Our problem is like my dog's – if he is contemplating and considering the proper boundary, he does really well, but if he is running full steam at a boundary, the correction doesn't stop him from blowing right through the boundary and into danger. That is why the Scriptures remind us to "keep in step" with the Spirit.

Since we live by the Spirit, let us keep in step with the Spirit. Galatians 5:25

19. You look funny

After we shear our sheep, a curious thing always happens. They begin picking on each other. These are the same animals that have shared a peaceful enclosure all year. Only now do they begin to ram each other unmercifully, as if to say, "You look funny!" And that begets more insults, as the other rams back with, "No, *you* look funny." Of course, none of them realizes they *all* look funny, now that they are shorn of their wool.

This reminds me of Jesus' admonition to make sure you have removed the plank from your own eye before you try to tell someone else about their problems. So next time you go to make fun of someone else or show them how foolish they are, you may wish to look in the mirror first!

"Why do you look at the speck of sawdust in your brother's eye and pay no attention to the plank in your own eye? How can you say to your brother, 'Let me take the speck out of your eye,' when all the time there is a plank in your own eye? You hypocrite, first take the plank out of your own eye, and then you will see clearly to remove the speck from your brother's eye." Matthew 7:3-5

20. A second chance

The peace of Christmas evening was quickly shattered by a screech of brakes, a thump and then painful squeals. We ran outside to see what had happened (or actually, to to sadly confirm what we somehow already *knew* had occurred): Brindle, our newly adopted little dog, had been playing in the road and had gotten ran over by a car. She was bleeding and her stomach was bright red but she was still alert as we rushed her to the emergency room vet. To our amazement, Brindle survived with only some relatively minor injuries. She had to wear a "cone of shame" for a while, but otherwise she was fine.

Now, Brindle knew that playing in the road was against the rules, not because we didn't want her to have any fun but because we knew it could kill her. She had played in the road previously and had big fun chasing cars until we would make her quit. This Christmas night she probably thought would be no different, then whack! Brindle could have died that night but thankfully was given another chance to learn from her mistakes.

Like Brindle, we think we can handle the dangerous fun of playing outside of God's guidance, but it is just a matter of time before the pain of our disobedience strikes us and we end up wearing a "cone of shame" or perhaps worse. Brindle has so far made the most of her second chance. How about you?

The Lord is not slow in keeping his promise, as some understand slowness. Instead he is patient with you, not wanting anyone to perish, but everyone to come to repentance. But the day of the Lord will come like a thief. The heavens will disappear with a roar; the elements will be destroyed by fire, and the earth and everything done in it will be laid bare. Since everything will be destroyed in this way, what kind of people ought you to be? You ought to live holy and godly lives. II Peter 3:9-11

21. Remorse

It was going to be a great day. It was a beautiful, warm, fall morning and we had so many fun things planned. However, we were running late. That got everybody on edge, rushing around hollering about all we needed to get done. At last, we were headed down the road, only to have to turn around because we forgot something at the house.  Now we were even *later*, which brought more bickering.

When everyone was back in the car, I sped out of the driveway, not even noticing that my sweet, arthritic, canine friend of 13 years had laid down near the car. With a thump and a squeal, it was all over. In a blink of an eye, my hasty actions had killed my faithful friend. Now getting somewhere in a rush didn't seem so important. Why didn't I look? Why didn't I slow down? Why did it have to be Buck? Why did it have to be me?

Guilt and remorse are heavy burdens. Nothing I can do will bring my friend back. However, through God's mercy and forgiveness, we can be better, we can learn from bad decisions, we can help others to slow down and avoid the senseless bickering that causes such tragic harm.

Don't have anything to do with foolish and stupid arguments, because you know they produce quarrels. And the Lord's servant must not be quarrelsome but must be kind to everyone, able to teach, not resentful. II Timothy 2:23,24

Weak #4 -- FEAR

Perhaps the most insidious weakness is fear. We know we should be content with all God has provided, and we know that we are not the center of the universe, and we know that disobeying God is not good but it is this fourth weakness -- fear -- that above all prevents us from truly experiencing the power of the Living God in our lives.

22. What were you created to do?

I had a little duck named Daisy that I had raised from birth for the farm's petting zoo. She spent the first part of her life waddling around inside the barn, eating, sleeping, playing with the other animals and sipping water from a little mason jar container. From all I could see, she was happy and content with her life inside the barn. However, the day I took her to the pond, her life changed forever. Timid at the edge of the large body of water, she was nervous at first about entering, but then she put one foot in and then the other. Soon she was gleefully and gracefully gliding and diving in, on, under and through the water. Daisy came alive and began to use all of what she was created to do.

Like Daisy, we go through life just getting little sips of God (just enough to keep us going), but when we are confronted with the ability to be totally immersed and supported by Him – it is a little scary – but only when we fully join God in His plans can we begin to enjoy all that we were created to be.

Love the Lord your God with all your heart and with all your soul and with all your mind and with all your strength. Mark 12:30

23. Got sheared!

Mary was a beautiful Dorset sheep who had been at our farm for more than 10 years. She knew when it got to be shearing time at our Spring Festival. As I approached, instead of the normal greeting, she would

 run away from me and try to hide. Once I had her in my grasp, she would try with all her might to break free. She would baaa and carry on something awful until she was on her backside and the clippers were at work. During the shearing process, Mary was completely silent and docile as if she finally remembered that this was for her benefit when the hot days of summer arrived.

Like Mary, we often run from God's pruning of the excesses in our lives. We hide and carry on hoping to avoid the shearing, but it is that surrender to the Master's hand that allows us to better face the days ahead.

He was oppressed and afflicted, yet he did not open his mouth; he was led like a lamb to the slaughter, and as a sheep before its shearers is silent, so he did not open his mouth. Isaiah 53:7

24. Getting the quills to lay down

Snuggles was a cute little African pygmy hedgehog that we raised in our home. Their entire head and back are completely covered in sharp quills, and what most people don't realize is that the hedgehog has a soft, fuzzy belly underneath. The defense mechanism of a hedgehog is to roll into a ball and stick out its pointy quills in all directions -- ouch! You never get to see and feel that soft underbelly until, through patient and non-threatening interaction, you have convinced them that you can be trusted.

Many people around us are like the hedgehog -- so afraid that they will be hurt, the only thing they show is their prickly barbs. To get the quills to relax and expose the softer side, we must first earn their trust.

Now it is required that those who have been given a trust must prove faithful. I Corinthians 4:2

25. Protector

Buck was a beautiful brown and white mix of a
collie and German shepherd. He was big and strong.
When our relationship was young, we would walk in the
woods and he would protect me from anything that
dared to move. But as the years went by, I began to
regard him as simply a nice, docile friend. One day I
went outside to find Buck staring at a large groundhog
that was lying in his bed, no longer prone to fighting.
Buck appeared to be just observing the intruder.
Thinking I would come to Buck's rescue, I got a stick
and tried to intimidate the groundhog into leaving but as
soon as I poked it, the groundhog came charging right at
me. Before I could even react, Buck sprang to alert. He
caught the groundhog in midair and shook it to
lifelessness before my eyes. I was amazed. I had
forgotten about Buck's role as a protector.

Sometimes we treat Jesus like I regarded Buck – a
nice, docile friend – and forget about the power of our
Lord who says, "I will protect you."

*If you say, "The LORD is my refuge," and you make the
Most High your dwelling, no harm will overtake you, no disaster
will come near your tent. For he will command his angels
concerning you to guard you in all your ways; they will lift you up
in their hands, so that you will not strike your foot against a stone.
You will tread on the lion and the cobra; you will trample the great
lion and the serpent. "Because he loves me," says the LORD, "I
will rescue him; I will protect him, for he acknowledges my name.
He will call on me, and I will answer him; I will be with him in
trouble, I will deliver him and honor him. Psalm 91:9-15*

26. Boo who

When my mama llama birthed her second cria, joy quickly turned to sadness. The back right leg of the new

solid-white baby llama just hung limp like a spaghetti noodle. It could not stand to nurse and instead just flailed around miserably crying out to its nervous mother. Our vet came out and helped us come to the same grievous conclusion: the baby should be euthanized to end its suffering. However, as we were preparing for the sad event, a school tour came down the road to visit the farm. And as we paused to let them pass, we noticed that it wasn't just any average school tour. This was a special education class with several handicapped children using walkers and wheelchairs. They marveled at the new baby and commented on how beautiful he was before proceeding down the road with their tour.

There would be no euthanasia today. None of us had the heart to do it that day. My vet used a wooden stick and bandage tape to create a makeshift splint/leg for the llama and said he would be back at the beginning of the next week to finish the job – if the baby was still living. We spent all weekend caring for the poor little creature. When Monday came, the little fellow had perked up. The vet took off the splint and one pretty little llama started running around. His leg had completely healed! Amazing. I often call Boo (all-white, born on Halloween) my "miracle llama" and tell people, "Miracles aren't just for people." It certainly had a profound effect on me and my vet. God is amazing. Boo went on to become one of the most famous and favored animals at our farm, giving kisses to all who visit.

You are the God who performs miracles; you display your power among the peoples. Psalm 77:14

27. Is love still possible?

Brindle was the scraggly, emaciated drop-off we adopted after a brutal winter storm. She weighed only 7 pounds when we took her to the vet the first time. Because of her obvious background of abuse, she was extremely skeptical, but also oh so much wanted to be loved. Her tail wagged enthusiastically when we approached, but when we reached our hand toward her, she instinctively cowered. Many months of tender, loving care later, Brindle would become a healthy 23-pound wonderful addition to our family.

Have you suffered abuse or just feel scraggly and unbeautiful? The Master is waiting to bring you in, provide for you and love you.

He has taken me to the banquet hall, and his banner over me is love. Song of Solomon 2:4

28. When no one seems to know what you are going through

A little boy ran into the farm office saying, "The new llama is here!"

"What new llama?" we said.

The boy led us out to the pasture where, sure enough, Crystal, our mama llama, had given birth to a healthy baby that  we named for the little boy who discovered the new arrival: Aiden. Crystal had been pregnant for 12 months and even though we fed and interacted with her every day during that period, none of us had a clue of what she was going through.

There is a great passage in Job where God reminds us that though we are oblivious to our surroundings, God is watching over even the tiniest detail, counting the months until a forest fawn is born. As an animal lover I revel in this passage where God expresses His care and concern for the animals. But it also reminds me of His great love for all of His creation. Like Crystal, you may feel that no one knows or understands what you are going through, but God does and He is counting the days till your joy may be realized.

"Do you know when the mountain goats give birth? Do you watch when the doe bears her fawn? Do you count the months till they bear? Do you know the time they give birth? They crouch down and bring forth their young; their labor pains are ended. Job 39:1-3

IN SUMMARY

The Creator has made us a little lower than the angels, but yet most of the time we end up acting worse than a bunch of common barnyard animals. We're rarely satisfied, we can think of only ourselves and we blatantly disobey our Master. Above all, we fear everything but the One whom is to be feared. To the malcontent, He is the provider; to the selfish, He is the Sacrifice; to the disobedient, He is the forgiveness; to the fearful, He is the Protector. Thankfully, God, our loving, Good Shepherd, knows each of us by name and knows each of our weaknesses, but He also knows each one of our capabilities and the plan He has for making our lives thrive in, through and beyond the Barnyard!

REFLECTIONS
BY MIKE PERRY

LIFE IN "THE GOOD OLD DAYS"

Have you ever wondered why so many people want
to glamorize or romanticize the "Good Old Days" and
talk about them in such a way as to clearly reflect their
desire to somehow go back or capture something they
feel missing in their lives today? However, if you
attempt to determine what they are looking for or what
they believe was better in those days, their answers
usually are illusive.

It is also interesting to attempt to determine upon
what experiences or actual knowledge they have reached
these determinations. Ordinarily, they have no personal
experience or firsthand knowledge from conversations
with people who actually *lived* during those days. Dig
further and you usually discover the "Good Old Days"
idea comes from reading novels and watching television
and movies. TV shows like "Little House on the
Prairie" and "The Waltons" are good examples. These
shows, particularly "Little House on the Prairie," do a
relatively good job of showing certain aspects of life
without all our modern conveniences.

However, have you ever given much thought to what life would *really* have been like back then?

Picture waking up in your log house on a cold winter morning before daylight without central heat and a thermostat set to keep the house toasty. Instead of getting out of bed and putting your feet on warm carpeted floors, your log house would not be much warmer than outside and the floor very cold. The bed and floor, particularly in the loft area of the cabin where the children sleep, might be sprinkled with snow blown in through the holes in the chinking between the logs. The house is quite cold because the fire in the fireplace had died down after being *banked* the night before. That means covering it with enough ashes so, hopefully, you can restart it in the morning by removing the ashes and adding kindling and wood which you prepared and stored nearby before going to bed.

To begin their long day, earliest risers – the mother and father, usually -- would start the fire in the fireplace and later in the wood cook stove in the kitchen. Children would hurry to the meager heat to dress and get ready to start their day as well. Remember, their day wouldn't begin with going to an indoor bathroom, perhaps with an electric heating fan and using the indoor toilet, taking a hot shower, brushing teeth with running water or combing or brushing hair in front of a lighted mirror. No, imagine having to go outside to use the privy or to heat the water on the stove or in the fireplace to have a little warm water to perhaps wash off a bit.

And *where* did the water come from? There was no indoor plumbing. Water had to come from a nearby creek or from a well that had been dug by hand by the father and the older boys -- all hard and dangerous work.

Water, from whichever source, had to be carried into the house in buckets, which also were handmade. Ask yourself: could *you* make a bucket out of wood tight enough to hold water? And water didn't always cooperate. During the winter, it often was frozen and had to first melt and be heated on the fire.

Let's go back to getting dressed. Do you imagine much time was spent going through their walk-in closets deciding what clothes to wear and which different outfit best suited their desired appearance for the day? Where did the clothes come from and how many different choices did they have? Picture yourself having to make your own clothes. Not just sewing the material – that was hard enough – but also having to make the *material* itself. It's hard for me to comprehend how much time and effort it had to have taken in shearing the sheep, cleaning and carding the wool, spinning it, dying it, weaving it and finally sewing it. You would have been fortunate to have more than one of anything to wear, and your clothes often were very worn and covered with patches. And perhaps your clothes would have been made from feed sacks. That was done not many years ago. What about shoes? Where did the leather come from? How was it prepared? Imagine trying to sew through leather to make moccasins or shoes.

The log house you lived in would be dark. No electric lamp by the bed or ceiling lights operated by a switch. Our early ancestors used candles. They also had to make their own wicks and candles. But that's another story.

Instead, let's hurry to breakfast. Don't be in *too* big of a hurry, because there are chores to do before we eat. Chickens, horses, cows, pigs and other animals all must be watered and fed before you are. There will be more carrying of water, after thawing it, if it's winter. And the trips to the barnyard would be in the dark. Imagine how happy you would be to have just kerosene lanterns to see by, instead of those earlier handmade candles.

Okay, *now* it's time for breakfast. Mother and the older girls would have been busy cooking on the wood-heated cast iron stove, if the family were fortunate enough to have one. Fire had to be started. What did they cook? What they ate in the winter depended mostly on how well the family had prepared during the summer and fall seasons. Remember, our ancestors had no stores at which to purchase food; they had to make everything themselves, or do without it. (Country stores – where families could buy a few food items like salt and sugar and perhaps flour if there was not a grist mill nearby to grind their wheat – eventually would come into being, but only after enough new settlers arrived to make the store commercially viable.) Another problem for the earliest settlers was they had no refrigerator to keep food from spoiling. To preserve food, they could dry it, smoke it, can it or bury it. Still, a mother whose family had worked hard in the summer and fall could provide a marvelous breakfast with everything coming from their farm, such as fresh eggs, ham, bacon, sausage, biscuits, pancakes with syrup, fried potatoes and milk. How satisfying it must have felt to be eating the fruits of your hard labor. But in harder times, breakfast also might have been only heated oats, mush or corn cakes.

The home where all this happens was often a log cabin that the settlers made from the huge trees they were cutting down to clear the land to create space to plant fields and gardens. The felled trees were hewed and shaped into logs of various lengths to build the house. Can you imagine building not only your own house, but the furniture too? And the house would be built to grow, as more log rooms would be added as the family increased. Only years later, after water-powered saw mills sprang up, might you build a house that looked more like our homes today.

Yes, it is mind boggling to think how industrious and creative we would need to be in order to live in the "Good Old Days" of our ancestors. And our day has only just begun.

Depending on the season, many things need to be done. Young children will walk to school where all the students, first grade to the eighth grade, are in one room with only one teacher. Older children work at home, helping with the jobs to feed and clothe the family; care for the animals; plow, sow, hoe and harvest the fields and gardens; build and mend the fences; cut and store hay; cut, split and stack firewood; carry and heat water to wash the clothes; make lye soap and candles; make quilts and blankets for the beds; braid rugs for the floors from rags; make and fix tools and wooden buckets and tubs; repair harness for the horse; shoe the horse; clean out the animal stalls and barn, saving the manure to fertilize the gardens; care for the babies and for the sick, since there was no doctor or hospital. The jobs were endless and there was never enough time.

Instead of envying them, you may now start feeling sorry for our ancestors. It sounds like they had no fun at all -- that their life was pure drudgery.

Well, while it was hard work, some aspects of their lives we *should* envy today. They worked and played together. They needed each other. They were family.

Everyone was important. Each was responsible for specific jobs, regardless of age. Everyone belonged. Not only did they work together, but also played, sang and danced together. To each new generation, they passed along the music and dance of their forefathers. They played and even made their musical instruments, like the fiddle, banjo and dulcimer, and taught the children to do the same. They went to church together, barn dances and house raisings as new neighbors arrived and a town ultimately was born. Together they made sweet things – molasses, maple syrup, applebutter – and life was good and shared.

But it also could be dangerous and often short, without modern medicines. It's hard to imagine facing epidemics and plagues and devastating diseases without doctors and hospitals. Imagine being confronted with a seriously ill child and trying to remember what your mother taught you about making home remedies from plants, roots and herbs. Think about the difficulties of childbirth or tending to very sick animals that are essential to keeping food on the table.

No, "the Good Old Days" were really not so good. Few of us would want to return to those times. We should never forget these settlers and what they did and endured to give us a quality of life we often take for granted today. We need to pledge to preserve our rich heritage and to share it with our children and grandchildren. It is a legacy that will enable them to enjoy that full rich abundant life intended for them by their Creator. Teach them the important lessons and values of life, the importance of being self-sufficient, determined, courageous and perseverant.

Upon further reflection on those marvelous television shows like "The Waltons" and "Little House on the Prairie," I think: who would not want to have parents and grandparents so wise and understanding? Who would not want to be raised in such beautiful environments, surrounded by such unconditional love and encouragement? Some of us were fortunate enough to have such experiences growing up, but most perhaps did not.

However, there *is* a happy ending. It is possible to have the best of both worlds. We can have all the advantages of our modern world without losing the important lessons from our past. Our rich heritage teaches us the need to belong and be a part of a family, to have meaningful and satisfying work, to love and be loved, to give and to receive, to teach and be taught, and to not only work but also sing and dance. As we've seen here, our ancestors knew the value of developing your creative nature, to be willing to learn something new. Don't take people and things for granted, and never forget to count all your blessings and thank your Heavenly Father each day for the life and opportunity He has permitted you to have.

CHANGE

I've always heard that nothing is certain in life but "death and taxes." I propose adding one more: the inevitability of change.

Nothing remains the same for long. Consider our physical bodies. We grow from babies to small children to teen-agers to adults. We go from crawling, to walking, to running, to climbing, to jumping, going faster and longer. Then it happens. It reverses. We get slower and slower, finding it ever more difficult to move. We stop jumping and running and begin to walk slower and with less certainty. We are no longer as strong or quick and can't see as well. Life steadily reminds us that our bodies have changed and so have we.

The same inevitable change occurs in every aspect of our world. One of life's greatest challenges is dealing with these changes. In fact, how much we enjoy life is greatly determined by how we deal with changes around us, changes in technology, communication, transportation and power/energy. Successful living requires that we adjust, learn about new things and acquire new skills. The consequences of not coping and adapting to our ever-changing environment can be quite significant. Imagine driving a horse and buggy and mailing hand-written letters while trying to exist in today's global economy with all its technological advancements providing instant access to most regions of the world 24 hours a day. It might work for a few people in limited situations, but for most of us it would be disastrous.

My 99-year-old mother-in-law, Virginia Mylar, has experienced changes from horse and buggies to Model T Fords, to steam trains, to buses, to jet airplanes, to watching moon landings and space launches on televisions. She witnessed the beginning of radio, crank telephone and now watches her great grandchildren use wireless handheld devices to talk, text and email friends, to play games, to watch movies, to take pictures and to record people in action. She has seen television go from a small black-and-white screen with an hour or two of broadcasting a day on a single channel to a huge color screen and hundreds of channels broadcasting 24 hours a day. She went from large complex antennas mounted on roofs and chimneys to cable to satellite.

But transportation and communication are not the only big changes she has seen in her life. The changes she has experienced in her lifetime are mind boggling. The medical improvements available today are hard to comprehend. None of her four children was born in a hospital and each was raised without most of the modern medicines, antibiotics and vaccines we now take for granted. There were no heart transplants or bypass surgeries or knee, hip and other replacement procedures available until much later in her life (and she has been fortunate to not need any of them). What about eye surgeries and lens implants, hearing aids and their improvement? The medical improvements available today are hard to comprehend.

Consider too the changes she has seen in her home and the various appliances she did not have to assist her in cooking, cleaning and laundering. Think about what she felt the first time she had running water or what she thought about going from a scrub board with homemade lye soup to a modern washing machine. Or from hanging wet clothes on a line outside to a dryer. Or from using a wood stove to the microwave, the ice box to the refrigerator, the fireplace to central heating with a thermostat and open windows without screens to air conditioning. When she was a young mother, homemaking meant keeping a garden and canning and preserving food, long before refrigeration and today's mega shopping centers with fresh fruits, vegetables, meats and fish from all over the world?

These are just *some* of the changes during this wonderful woman's life. And she would be the first to say that, while these improvements have made things easier and quicker, that does not always mean life is better. In many respects, these changes also have affected how people made their livings and supported their families. Men left the farms in large numbers to work in factories and businesses to make and sell these new products. They often moved to new communities and states where the jobs were available and drastically changed the lives of their families in the process. Those moves and changes have continued as the manufacturing process has changed with more and more use of machinery and computerized equipment which does the work that used to require thousands of men. Advancements in transportation, technology and communication have also expanded the competition for these jobs all over the world resulting in thousands of people losing their jobs in our country as new jobs are created in China and other foreign countries. In other words, change almost always has more than one component, good and bad, intended and unintended. Even determining what *is* good often depends on to whom you are talking.

Consider the Linotype machine. It was invented by Ottmar Mergenthaler in the late 1800s and had 15,000 moving parts. An engineering marvel of its time – "the eighth wonder of the world," many said – it revolutionized printing and greatly reduced the cost of producing newspapers, books and magazines to make them more readily available to more people for less money. It set type for printing much faster than people doing it by hand. Everyone proclaimed the progress.

Hold on. Not everyone.

Thousands of men who had previously made livings setting type by hand were eventually losing their jobs. Each Linotype machine replaced four or five typesetters. One of the typesetters could learn to use the new machine and maybe another could learn to maintain it. That would mean a net loss of three or four jobs per new machine at the print shop. On the other hand, nationwide the new machine created many more new jobs than it eliminated. People were hired to manufacture the machine, supply the iron and other components, transport it, repair it, provide the lead, gas and electricity to operate it. Of course, this was of little consolation to the original typesetters who had lost their jobs in the town where their print shop was located. Their options were to be retrained, find other jobs in the town or move to where the new jobs were being created.

Before you feel sorry for the typesetters who lost their jobs, ask yourself how many people you know today who operate Linotype machines for a living. Computers and technology eliminated their jobs the same way they eliminated the typesetter's jobs.

While we have focused on how change has affected individuals at home and work, companies and businesses likewise are impacted by change, both positively and negatively. For evidence you need look no further than Mergenthaler Linotype Co. of New York, USA, the firm that manufactured and sold the Linotype machine. The company prospered for many years as did their employees, suppliers and the communities where they were located. As time passed, technology improved. New discoveries and inventions created even better and faster and, yes, cheaper ways to set type and the manufacturing company had to adjust. Why? It made one great product, but that is not enough to sustain a company in today's competitive world. It must constantly restructure itself and find new and better products to make and sell or merge and become a part of a larger company, which happened to Mergenthaler.

And what happens when a company doesn't anticipate change? We have an example right here in my hometown of Huntington, West Virginia. As I was growing up in the 1950s, Houdaille Industries made some of the world's finest steel chrome bumpers for cars. Bumpers were massive steel devices on the front and rear of cars that absorbed much of the damage when cars collide -- particularly at lower speeds or when parking. Today Houdaille is no longer around. The company did not go out of business because someone made a better or even cheaper bumper. Instead, bumpers themselves changed due to concerns for better gas consumption and fuel economy. Bumpers began to be made of lightweight plastic with more emphasis on looks than preventing damage. Houdaille failed to anticipate change.

There are thousands of similar stories around the country. Many years ago, bottles were hand blown by craftsmen at glass plants. There were several in Huntington. Then along came Mike Owens of Point Pleasant, West Virginia, who invented a process to enable glass bottles to be manufactured in molds. It was significantly faster and cheaper than bottles made by hand. Owens-Illinois was a company that grew from that idea. It resulted in thousands of new jobs being created, but at the same time many glass-blowing jobs were lost. Fortunately more jobs were created in Huntington and elsewhere than were lost. However, in my lifetime, along came plastic and new technology; now there is no longer an Owens Illinois in my community and all of their employees lost their jobs and their suppliers lost a big customer, meaning they needed fewer employees. Except this time the new jobs created by the plastic industry were not in my hometown or state and maybe not even in this country. There were more jobs perhaps in the world, but not in this country and certainly not in my community.

Change and the consequences of change is good and bad, a lesson learned, a lesson often forgotten. Unfortunately, losing good manufacturing jobs affects everyone. As the population declines and ages, it also costs the jobs of the people who previously serviced the manufacturer -- employees, the grocery, car salesmen, banks, clothing stores and many other retailers.

Come to Heritage Farm Museum & Village and see how our lives have changed over the last 150 years and how much we take for granted the wonderful quality of life we enjoy today. Learn the need to prepare for the future, of adapting to change and the realization that it is inevitable with both its good and negative consequences. As employees we discover the importance of lifelong learning and the constant need to be retrained and to develop new skills as we compete with people all over the world, not just locally. Perhaps most important as executives, managers, board members and other leaders of companies, business professionals, schools, churches, hospitals and universities, etc., we need to be reminded and never forget the consequences of not anticipating or fostering change. Remember the leaders of the Linotype, Houdaille or Owens-Illinois. At Heritage Farm Museum & Village, you will see a chart showing 2,600 manufacturers of automobiles in the United States, examples of 100 washing machines out of over 1,000 companies who have manufactured them, as well as maps showing hundreds of different railroads in West Virginia and Ohio, not counting coal and lumber companies. What happened to all these companies and why? Come to the Museum and learn about these companies and the winners and losers. Are you adequately preparing for the future of your organization? Consider doing strategic planning at the Museum in one of our several facilities and take a tour of the museums and exhibits as you examine your future by reflecting upon the past and the many lessons that can be learned from it.

ENTREPRENEURSHIP

Entrepreneur, *noun, a person who organizes and manages a business or industrial undertaking. An entrepreneur takes the risk of not making a profit and gets the profit when there is one.*

The problem is more difficult than spelling or defining. We hear the word used frequently and many important organizations are attempting to determine how to foster it and cause more people in our society to become one. Colleges and universities are developing programs to teach people how to be one. Many "how-to" books have been published. Our president and other leaders in our nation's capital and many governors around the country describe the need for them to be a major ingredient to solve the great economic challenges facing our country.

They are responsible for the economic prosperity of our nation in the past and its hope for its future. Many people dream of becoming one, but few are willing to try because the risks of failure are large. There are no age, gender or nationality limitations. Everyone is welcome to become one, but few do so. It is often more important to know how much you are willing to lose instead of how much money you have. Some have been rich but most have been poor or with only a small amount of money. Who are these people?

Entrepreneurs.

In trying to define an entrepreneur, it may be helpful to explain what it is not. It is not necessarily a manager of a company or even a chairman or chief executive officer of a very successful business. They are responsible for the business but did they start it? It is not necessarily an inventor or an individual doing research discovering something new. It is not necessarily *the idea person* who individually spawns new concepts or processes. All of these people are important parts of the development of a successful business. Some are important at the beginning, during and even at the end but the true entrepreneur is there from beginning to end.

Entrepreneurs are the driving force from the very beginning that not only take the financial risk to bring an idea, concept or product to market, but also actively organize and manage the process through to the end. They bear the risk of not making a profit and they get the profit when there is one. There are investors, individuals, funds and groups who risk money on someone else's idea, concept or invention, but it is not theirs. They are often very important and vitally needed by many entrepreneurs, but by my definition, these are not entrepreneurs themselves. There may be bankers or other lenders or even partners who take risks in exchange for potential profits, but they are not entrepreneurs since the creative nature of the idea, service or potential product was not theirs. There may be professionals and managers who are of invaluable assistance. All of these various people are important and maybe even vitally needed but they are not entrepreneurs.

For the entrepreneur to be successful, it normally requires a total commitment of all of his or her time, energy, resources and blood, sweat and tears. Others may be involved, but the ultimate risk of success and failure rests on his or her shoulders and abilities. Ever wonder why many ideas, concepts or inventions are sold or assigned to someone else? It's because the original individual is not willing to assume or accept that total risk of failure and accepts a specific price or percentage of profits, if any, in lieu thereof. They may continue to be involved, but with limited or no risk, and thus, they cease to be entrepreneurs. This is not a criticism, only an observation. We vitally need these creative people with their unique and wonderful abilities. They just are not entrepreneurs. We also need the individuals and companies who acquired the rights to the original idea, concept or product and stand in the stead of the original inventor and now accept the financial risks and rewards to complete the process and bring something to the marketplace.

What does it take to be an entrepreneur? Is it something that simply can be taught and learned? The answers to the questions are not easy and are quite controversial.

To be an entrepreneur, one must be creative. Where do the ideas, concepts and new or improved products come from? An entrepreneur must be self-confident and willing to take calculated and carefully identified risks. An entrepreneur must often be able to communicate the dream to other people and gain their confidence and support to make it a reality. An entrepreneur must be disciplined and willing to often make sacrifices and adjust priorities in life to achieve success.

I don't believe you just suddenly wake up and decide to be an entrepreneur nor do I think it as easy as just going to school to become one. Obviously a good education can be extremely important but it is not essential, as a study of past successful entrepreneurs will show.

I think you'll agree we need more entrepreneurs to stimulate our economy, create jobs, create wealth, pay taxes and make charitable contributions, and it is important we attempt to create more of them.

But how?

There are many different approaches and the government and many foundations make large financial investments in attempting to find answers.

I believe it must start with encouraging our children to be creative and self-confident. This may sound easy but, in fact, many children lack confidence in themselves and unfortunately some others have too much of it. Confidence can be inappropriate and misguided. It is a delicate balance, not too little and not too much, particularly if misplaced.

At Heritage Farm Museum & Village, we believe it is important to make sure the children of Appalachia gain a more positive self-image. (As defined by the Appalachian Region Commission, Appalachia is composed of portions of 12 states and the entire state of

West Virginia for a total of 13 states, with 420 counties of which 82 are still described as economically distressed. A significant percentage of those distressed counties are within several hours drive of Huntington, West Virginia.) However, it is hard to develop self-confidence if you lack self-esteem. Too many people have told and described these children and their parents in such uncomplimentary and even derogatory terms that many have come to believe it.

Ironically, at a time when it is regarded as unacceptable behavior to demean people because of their race, color, nationality, gender or sexual preference, it is permissible for political leaders, media pundits, comedians and others to make fun of the people of Appalachia and their ancestors. Such behavior on a wide scale in the popular media, television, movies and the press has significantly undermined the self-image of the children of Appalachia. How can they be expected to develop positive self-esteem and self-confidence under these circumstances? No such misconduct would be permitted against our Native Americans, or African-Americans or various ethnic immigration groups or religious groups like the Muslims, but the "Hillbillies of Appalachia" are fair gain. Hard to understand why.

But that is a separate issue, discussed here only as background for understanding the special challenges facing the children of Appalachia and encouraging them to become entrepreneurs to help break the economic downturn or spiral in their home communities and regions. No one is in as good a position as these children if properly nurtured and encouraged to become the future business men and women of their communities, people wanting to get ahead and make a difference and willing to work hard and take risks to do so.

In fact, if these children knew more about their proud Appalachian heritage and culture, they would realize how self-confident and determined their ancestors were when they came across the mountains into what today is Appalachia. They would learn to appreciate the dreams of their ancestors to be self-sufficient, proud and independent people, building their own homes, raising and providing their own food and clothing in a very hostile environment. This is the one of the driving forces behind the creation of Heritage Farm: to instill in Appalachian school children a better appreciation of their heritage and of the remarkable people, their ancestors, who have given us this marvelous quality of life we often take for granted today. Hopefully, when they realize what their ancestors accomplished through hard work and perseverance, they will likewise dream big dreams and be willing to work harder to make those dreams a reality. Maybe when they realize it was their ancestors who started the country stores, the saw mills and grist mills, and later the coal and timber companies and even railroads, they will learn to aspire to bigger things and accomplishments themselves. We are committed to helping them appreciate their rich heritage and culture and perhaps dreaming bigger dreams of what they can accomplish by emulating their ancestors and learning to be confident in their own abilities and willing to risk failure or gain success by relying upon their own confidence and determination.

COUNTRY STORE

The country store sold a little of everything. It was the center of the economic, political and often social activities of the area. For many years in the development of Appalachia, there were no stores. There were generally not enough people living near each other and

there would not have been enough products available that people could afford to buy or barter and trade for. The lonely peddler filled the void, walking into a remote area, carrying his back pack filled with small items the housewife or other family members might need and could not make themselves. A simple needle is a good example. If the wife lost her needle, it would have been almost impossible to make or replace and she would have been unable to sew new clothes, patch old ones or prepare quilts for the winter to keep her family warm. She would not have money to buy the needle, and so she would barter. Perhaps she could trade some yarn she had spun or cloth she had woven or maybe a fur or pelt that her husband had hunted and tanned. She also would have liked some indigo to help her dye her yarn a beautiful blue. She could use certain leaves, bark, berries and roots to get most colors, but a particular blue was difficult. The husband might have liked a pocketknife to replace the one he lost. He had no access to iron and his tools were limited to those he carried over the mountains himself or that he had made, primarily of wood, so the peddler was welcome.

Later the peddler, who had been on foot, would start using a horse to carry his wares and even later, a wagon. As the old saying goes, "He was a sight for sore eyes," not just for the wide array of items he carried, but perhaps almost as important as a source of news. We forget how isolated people were in the mountains. There were no newspapers and of course no radio, television or telephones. Mail was almost non-existent. When people left the East, it was very difficult to stay in touch with their families back home or to stay current on political affairs or military activities. The peddler would keep them informed on the latest national news, and even local news about their seldom-seen distant neighbors. He could even act as the mailman.

Later still, when more people lived in closer proximity, you might find a trading post which might later become the country store. Maybe the same peddler who knew the area would see an opportunity to settle down and decide to open a country store to serve his previous customers. As roads improved and buggies and wagons became more common, the peddler-turned-storekeeper had more and more customers.

Early products for sale were limited, but gradually began to increase as methods of transportation and roads improved and industrial activities increased in the East. Many early products had been handmade by local craftsmen and bartered and traded with the store operator for items they needed. Common items were wooden buckets, barrels, tubs, pitchforks, rakes, churns, brooms, spinning wheels and the like. Wool was also spun into yarn, dyed and woven into cloth material or coverlets that were also bartered and traded. Of course, all these handmade products were later replaced by machine-made products at lower prices. Barter and trade was still quite common, though, as money was scarce until banks became established in an area.

In fact, the country store operator himself often was the first banker as he determined to whom to extend credit until his customer was able to sell his crops or furs and pelts or animals to get cash to pay his bill. Extending credit was a risky business. It depended on customers' ability to keep a good name by paying their bills, even if the family otherwise had to cut back and do without what they wanted and maybe even needed. The risks – hard winters, droughts, too much rain, fires and illnesses – were substantial for everyone. Nowadays, when we get too much rain or not enough, we complain about our lawns, but for early settlers (and for today's farmers), it could be disastrous. No crops would often mean almost starving to death, not to mention the inability to pay debts at the store. It could also mean going back over the mountains to the East, admitting failure, or striking out further west for hopefully a new beginning but without anything. The hardships are unimaginable, but somehow through dogged determination, perseverance, tenacity, they made their dreams realities.

So, a good country store operator was a great asset to his community. He and his customers prospered or failed together. Theirs was a mutual dependency. Not only did customers need to keep good credit by paying their bills, but the merchant needed to sell quality goods at prices his customers could afford so that both benefited. The store operator needed to make a profit, not only to support himself and his family, but to be able to buy more merchandise and products to keep his inventory adequate and to offset the losses when people did not pay him. Prices also had to be reasonable to enable the customer to purchase what he needed and to sell his surplus food, pelts, animals, etc. in order to pay his bills at the store. This delicate balance sometimes was hard to achieve when there was only one store for many miles of difficult travel, which often resulted in high prices.

Fueling growth for communities and businesses was the improvements in transportation. As roads improved and new conveyances were introduced, more stores became available, which resulted in more competition. Merchants no longer had a monopoly. To compete, they had to offer more merchandise at lower prices and better service. Now with more than one choice, customers had to learn that lower prices did not always mean better or equal quality or even better service, like credit when times were difficult and they needed more time to pay. Relationships began to change. Sometimes longtime customers forgot the country store operator who had helped them through hard times in the past and were attracted by lower prices at a new store operator nearby.

In the early days of the development of the country store, it truly was a one-stop experience. It was in many respects the focal point of the community, where people found out what was going on in their towns and how their friends and neighbors were doing. The country store operator knew everyone and everyone knew him. It is hard to imagine his business being successful for long if he was not honest and trustworthy. He had to be firm but also had to be blessed with the skill to know when to extend credit and when to not. In many small communities, he was one of the important people in town, admired and respected along with the doctor and the preacher.

But change was constant and, as transportation improved and as more industrial goods and products were being manufactured and available for sale, the country store kept expanding and adding on more space to make room for all these new products. The clothing area became larger, as did the hardware section and the medicines. On and on it grew until one store couldn't hold it all. New stores started opening that only sold one product, like clothes and shoes, and in some instances, only for men or women. Hardware stores started being separate from grocery stores. Customers began to prefer to shop in these individual stores which often had a wider selection of goods in a more limited area and offered more personalized attention and services.

With time's passage, country store operators were finding it harder to compete. At the same time, a new competitor – catalogs – appeared with improved postal services and vastly better roads and rail lines. Taking advantage of improvements in the printing industry, companies like Sears and Montgomery Ward began mailing free catalogs with beautiful pictures of thousands of products from all over the world. Catalog items could be purchased and delivered from such distant places as Chicago and New York City. The end of the country store was in sight. In smaller communities and more remote areas, it lasted a little longer but ultimately it almost totally faded from the scene.

It is interesting that in more recent years we have witnessed the demise and gradual closing of these small specialty businesses, like the men's and women's clothing stores, groceries, hardware, drug stores, independent gas stations, various repair shops, etc. to see us going back to the idea of big one-stop stores, like Walmart, where you can get your eyes examined, do your banking and buy groceries, gas and millions of almost every other type of product manufactured in the world, including more and more from China. Perhaps one day we will see the re-emergence of small businesses and stores and their more personalized services and products aided by the computer and other electronic advances. Maybe handmade dresses sewn by seamstresses will become the style again. Remember, we have gone from times when all clothes were made by hand to store-bought clothes from a country store to clothing from specialty shops. Wouldn't it be interesting if the next stop is a return to handmade dresses as being the latest fashion? After all, that wouldn't be so different from the world of furniture, in which we have seen a return of the value of tables and chairs handmade by Appalachian craftsmen, not unlike our forefathers!

Who knows what will happen next? History has a way of repeating itself as people adapt to an ever-changing and smaller world. Come visit the Country Store at Heritage Farm Museum & Village and see for yourself how things have changed and imagine how different the future may be from our rich and historic past. Progress is interesting to watch. Be a participant in history -- not just an observer.

THE PIONEER WOMAN

I am awed by the remarkable pioneer woman. She was of necessity the glue that held the family together and also the center of much activity. Don't get me wrong -- she and her husband were a team and depended upon each other. Each was vital for not only survival but the quality of life their family did or did not enjoy. However, much has been written about the pioneer man and his rugged independence and the skills he had to possess to protect and provide for his family. It was primarily his strength and determination that was needed to cut and clear the trees to make room to plant gardens and fields for grain and food. It was his skill and resourcefulness to take those trees and hew them into logs in order to build a house for his family.

But I want to focus on the critical role of his wife in making that house a home, on what skills and qualities she needed and on what a normal day in her life must have looked like. I am not glamorizing or romanticizing this time in history or advocating returning to the so-called "Good Old Days." But by studying these people, we can learn some lessons and values that can help us today as we struggle with many similar issues and challenges in life.

Unfortunately, most of what we know about pioneer life comes from watching TV shows like "Little House on the Prairie," where the people are already in a warm log cabin enjoying abundant food they have grown or hunted and going to bed covered with beautiful handmade quilts listening to their father play his fiddle as he relaxes. On television, they are protected by a wonderful dog outside who is watching over them and their animals, horses, cows, sheep, pigs, chickens and geese. It is tranquil and calm and all is well on the frontier for the moment. However, we know from watching earlier episodes that will soon change and a new drama will unfold only to find our family safe and sound in the end due to the bravery of everyone, particularly the dog and sometimes the father.

No wonder people today long to return to those days surrounded by love, wisdom and acceptance.

However, where did these pioneers come from and how did they get there? We often fail to comprehend what it would have been like to leave our families and friends and the security of living in the towns and cities of the East. Life in the East was supported by the stores, crafts, businesses and commerce there as well as by the ships from Europe and the rest of the World that brought to the Atlantic ports their goods and products. When the early pioneers crossed into the mountains, it was a wilderness and in many respects more dangerous and uncertain than crossing the ocean by sailing ships. Often, they would never see or even hear from their families and friends again due to the difficulty of travel and lack of adequate postal services. On TV, we watched them travel by covered wagons, often in the security of groups accompanied by a wide variety of animals and supplies necessary for their new beginnings. In reality, the earliest settlers in our area did not enjoy covered wagons or even horses, except perhaps one or two to help carry their meager supplies. They walked. They slept outdoors, often in the rain protected by whatever was available like tents or a cave. They hunted, collected fruit and nuts and otherwise cooked and provided their own food as they traveled. Imagine how long it took. Imagine the anxious moments in the wilderness with snakes and wild animals and the fear of the Native Americans. These pioneers carried with them the barest necessities, such as a few cooking implements, axe, knives, flintlock rifle with lead and gun powder. Once they reached their destination, they knew they would have to make everything else they needed with their own hands. If they did not bring something with them or make it, they had to learn how to do without.

What about their destination? Some were going to a specific location, to land they had purchased from a land company or an individual who had received a land grant in exchange for military services. But often they were just looking for a good place to settle and try to claim ownership by possession.

And the big question is why. Why were they doing this? It was a hard, dangerous and long journey with nothing at the end of their travels but a lot of hard work and struggles to survive against what must have seemed like insurmountable challenges. What were they looking for and why?

Of course, each story is different, but there were certain common themes and characteristics. These people were looking for an opportunity, a new beginning. They had hopes and dreamed of a better tomorrow and were willing to work extremely hard and overcome unbelievable difficulties to bring their dreams to life. They accepted the risks in exchange for the rewards, something that was theirs, and for the knowledge that they had done it. There must have been satisfaction in knowing they provided for themselves and family, a home and a new life they had earned for themselves. These settlers were truly free and independent, beholding to no one. Proud, self-reliant, industrious, courageous and resourceful people, our ancestors. What a rich and noble heritage we have.

Most of our culture's stories focus on the man in these adventures, but let's try to understand what it was like for the woman, maybe even a new bride. What were the peculiar concerns she faced each day and each new season?

Imagine leaving your mother, sisters and friends and facing the challenges ahead, often without any help. Try to picture starting your day in a house with little or no heat, perhaps even with a little snow on your bed which had blown in through the cracks between the logs. You get dressed hurriedly in front of the fireplace or the wood cook stove in the kitchen, putting on clothes you made yourself, including the cloth and material itself. You rekindle the fire banked the night before, then answer nature's call either outside at the privy/outhouse or inside with the chamber pot or slop jar, which had to be emptied outside. Then you melt frozen water in the fireplace or on the stove to start preparing breakfast, the first of three full meals you'll prepare, cooking foods you helped raise and preserve without refrigeration. While it cooks, you help the children start their day, feeding the chickens, gathering eggs when available, maybe catching, killing and cleaning older hens to cook. You clean up after serving each meal only to start preparing the next one. In between, you sew, patch and mend clothes, saving scraps for braiding rugs and making quilts. In the spring and summer, you work in the garden. In the fall, you plant, hoe, weed and harvest crops, gathering and preserving the various roots, leaves and tonics needed to tend to the medical needs of the family when sickness arose. You also make candles for lighting, wash clothes using lye soap you made yourself, bake breads and pies, churn butter and make cheese. Did I mention the canning and preserving of fruits and vegetables to keep them from spoiling? The carrying water from the well or creek? The carding, spinning, dying and weaving wool and other materials like flax to make winter clothing for the family? Helping butcher the hog and smoking, salting and preserving the hams, bacon and other meats for the winter? Picking the fruit and making applebutter, apple cider, jellies and jams?

The list goes on and on. Many of the jobs and responsibilities arise from specific seasons and the weather, inside jobs and outside jobs, depending on whether it's raining or dry, hot or cold. Remember, there's no central heating systems, no air conditioning either, except for the occasional cool summer breeze.

Perhaps you'll be able to rest with family as the sun sets on another day, happy to be together and to have overcome whatever had to be done to not only survive, but dream of better days and a brighter future for you and your children. You collapse in bed at the end of the day with minimal privacy. It makes me exhausted just thinking about it. No vacations or sabbaticals and – surprising to us – few regrets.

No wonder the women of Appalachia were so remarkable. What a rich legacy has been passed down from them for future generations! It should be a great comfort to us to be reminded of our ancestors' accomplishments, because it reassures us that we can enjoy the same satisfaction if we never forget their lessons. Ours is a legacy of confidence and a dogged determination, one we can pass on to our children, a legacy of love for family, God and community which will enable them to enjoy a rich full abundant life.

While writing this, a vivid thought struck me that Henriella, my wife for more than 53 years, would have made a marvelous pioneer. She possesses the skills, talents, characteristics and attitudes of these remarkable early settlers, our Appalachian ancestors. Like they, she is industrious, creative, resourceful, determined and compassionate and -- perhaps most important -- possessing of an adventuresome spirit.

How else would you describe a lady whose idea it was to move from a beautiful brick home in the city with all the modern conveniences to a burnt-out log cabin without central heat, air conditioning, indoor plumbing or adequate electricity, with three children -- the oldest being 12 and the youngest 2? Yes, some people may use less flattering terms to describe such a woman, but looking back on that momentous decision, we have often reflected that it was one of the best decisions we ever made as a family. What a great atmosphere in which to raise a family, working together to make our home more livable, while enjoying and experiencing life on the farm with animals and gardens. Together we learned firsthand how much we had taken for granted the previous quality of life we enjoyed in the city.

Today almost 38 years later, that old log cabin is part of a beautiful house, but more importantly, a warm home that has helped nurture those three children now grown and married with children of their own. Those nearly four decades have been quite an adventure. When we started, we had only 90 days to work on the burnt cabin before we had to move in. We had spent our money from the sale of our house in the city to buy the 150-acre farm where the log cabin was located and did not have the funds to hire a contractor to help us.

After work and on Saturdays our family and fortunately some of our friends helped us at least make the cabin habitable. We put in a septic tank, an indoor bathroom, running water in the kitchen and a more adequate electrical service. We replaced the tin roof which was on top of hand-made wood shake shingles which had burnt. Our water came from a well and had too much iron and sulfur and smelled like rotten eggs. We heated the house with a cast iron stove in the living room with wood we split and carried in throughout the day. It heated us as we cut it, split it, carried it and finally as we burnt it. Talk about staying in shape! We did not have to go to the "Y" to work out or stay fit. I say "we" correctly because my wife and I and our children were all involved in every aspect of the work, either doing it or cleaning up. Cleaning up was a formidable challenge as some of the logs had been burnt as well and the other log walls had been covered with paper, cardboard and boards in an effort to keep bugs out and heat in with obvious poor results.

My pioneer wife never missed a day and participated in most of the activities as we read from books trying to learn how to be electricians, plumbers, carpenters and roofers. Thanks to family and friends we made it, but that was just the beginning of our marvelous experiences which has now resulted in the establishment of the Heritage Farm Museum & Village. As we worked on the house, we fell in love with the logs and began thinking about how it was built and who built it. Not the actual people themselves, but the early settlers in this region of Appalachia who built hundreds, maybe thousands of very similar log cabins. We developed an immense appreciation of these people and the hard work and determination it took to get the job done. Remarkable people – creative, resourceful, determined, industrious and even patient because nothing substantial happens very easily or quickly. These characteristics describe my beautiful wife to a "T".

Sound familiar? I am sure there is a pioneer woman in your life as well. Remarkable ladies, the product of a rich heritage passed down from generation to generation. Strong, capable, caring, creative, resourceful, industrious and yet tender and kind, full of love, compassion and concern for others, humble and always willing to help others. They were and are the backbone of our homes, our society and our future.

The future depends on this rich heritage being preserved by being passed down from one generation to the next. It only takes one generation failing to pass these attitudes and characteristics to the next generation to break this continual chain of progress with the past. Never let it be said that our generation or your generation failed to do so. The future is dependent upon us. Let us not fail our children and grandchildren. Don't worry about the skills of the past, like sewing, weaving, quilting, etc. as groups are working to preserve these crafts. They will not be lost. I am more concerned about passing on the characteristics and attitudes of our ancestors: confidence, independence, self-reliance, curiosity, willingness to take risks, adaptability to change. We want to pass on our ancestors' ability to dream big and work hard to make those dreams a reality. Our children and grandchildren must have these characteristics and attitudes to compete in a global economy against the best anywhere in the world and win. It will take self-confidence and self-esteem and a realization that if their ancestors were able to overcome unbelievable hardships to give us a quality of life we take for granted today, that the same blood flows in their veins. Our children must know they can do whatever they set their minds to do if they work as hard and determined as did their fabulous Appalachian ancestors.

ONE-ROOM SCHOOLHOUSE

Providing a free public education to the nation's children was one of the most important factors leading to the United States becoming an industrial world power. With it, we also became a nation of people from every walk of life, particularly the middle class, who rose from humble beginnings to invent, improve and mass produce an unbelievable variety of products that have changed the world and its people. The symbol of that education is perhaps best represented by the one-room schoolhouse.

It was just that, of course – one room occupied by students from the first grade to the eighth grade, both boys and girls, taught by one teacher. It's surprising how many people fondly remember attending a one-room schoolhouse, particularly in the rural parts of Appalachia. From talking to these former students, it's obvious they received a good education. Most attended only for a few years before their school became two rooms and then three, and more. Schools became larger with improvements in methods of transportation enabling children to get to and from school as more children began to live nearer each other. In other words, one-room schools did not disappear because they provided a poor education. On the contrary, they were often quite effective, obviously depending upon the quality of the teacher. But interestingly, the concept is still debated today -- smaller vs. larger schools.

The one-room schoolhouse was definitely small compared to today's mega-schools, some having a thousand students in only a few grades, with teachers teaching only one subject. To someone unfamiliar with the one-room school, it is almost impossible to believe that the concept had any merit. Most of us went to school in small classes with students our own age. In grade school the same teacher usually taught all the different subjects. As we graduated and went farther in school, we stayed in the same age group but started having different teachers for each different subject.

Now, imagine being in the sixth grade trying to learn geography as your ancestors did. In the same room, your teacher also is helping a first-grader learn to spell and print his name, a second-grader learn to read, a third-grader to do long division, a fourth-grader study history, a fifth-grader solve a math problem, a seventh-grader work on American literature and an eighth-grader recite the "Declaration of Independence." Actually, it would be more complicated than that, because there would be more than one student in the various grades, all learning at different levels and different speeds, some faster and higher, and others slower and lower. Doubt it or not, it did work. Many very successful people began their education in just such an environment.

No doubt part of the system's success was the realization by many students, but certainly not all, that education would change them. It could either transport them into an exciting new world away from their rural homes or enable them to stay home and become better and smarter farmers or whatever they wanted to become. In either instance, education would help them enjoy their lives to a greater extent. Another part of the one-room schoolhouse's success came from the support it received from the parents and other adults in the area, even those who had no children. Though many of our ancestors had little schooling themselves, they knew the importance of being able to read and write and do mathematics. They were willing to sacrifice to assure their children received as good an education as possible, to make sure their children did not waste this important opportunity.

A lesson we can take from this is that good education does not necessarily depend on how large or small classrooms should be, even making sure the classes are composed of students who understand why they need an education and students who are encouraged by their parents or that they must be taught by excellent and dedicated teachers. One can't help but think that it takes all three – the student, the parents and the teachers/administrators – working together to help us regain our world leadership position in the education of our children in a very competitive global economy, regardless of the size of the facilities. It is foolish to think the teachers can do it by themselves. Of course, they cannot. Students and their parents have to accept their vital responsibilities to make it happen and if we can get it right, watch out, world – America is back!

But let's not romanticize the one-room schoolhouse. It was often disrupted by older children who did not want to learn. And, unfortunately, there were also parents who did not see the importance of an education, thought it a waste of time, preferring to keep their children at home to help with the work. Some parents even imagined people were looking down upon them because of their own lack of education and did not want their children to "rise above them" or "get above their raising." They feared schooling would inspire their children to leave home with their fancy education. Sound familiar? Lack of parental support and encouragement is nothing new.

Let's also not forget the many stories of having to walk two miles to school in the winter in two feet of snow.

Uphill.

Both ways.

Okay, perhaps things were exaggerated a bit, but getting to and from school was difficult. And don't forget the one-room schoolhouse was often like most of the homes: heated in the winter by an iron stove with wood or coal carried in by the boys and in the summer cooled by opening the windows. Restrooms were outhouses -- outside toilets -- usually one for boys and one for girls, each with catalogs for toilet paper. Water was carried in from a well and poured into the drinking bucket from which everyone drank using the same cup or ladle. Water was also carried in and poured in a basin for washing.

The students' desks – usually facing pictures of George Washington and Abraham Lincoln behind the teacher's desk – were of different sizes with the very smallest for the first-grader being up front. The desks gradually got larger with the largest being in the rear of the classroom for the older students. In the earliest days of the one-room school there would not have been desks; instead, students sat on logs or benches. School books, slate, chalk and erasers as well as pens and ink also would have come along later. There would have been spelling bees, math contests, plays, recitations and many other educational activities along with everyone's favorite, even today -- recess.

Punishment of students was also quite different than today. At Heritage Farm Museum & Village, when we show the visiting school children our example of the one-room schoolhouse, a wooden paddle and a dunce cap are prominently on display. Among today's students, there is no recognition or fear of either. There is quite a different reaction from our older visitors, who vividly remember these instruments of punishment. On the other hand, younger guests groan at the mention of "time out" or -- even worse -- having to put their noses into a circle on the chalk board and stand in that position as punishment for some infraction of the rules. Obviously, whipping and other forms of corporal punishment are no longer permitted, feeding the ongoing debate as to the wisdom of not paddling, similar to no longer reading the Bible or saying a prayer to start the school day. It seems nothing in life remains the same very long. Many things change for the better and others for the worse with most people not agreeing which was better and which was worse. It certainly makes for interesting times and debates.

Meanwhile, then as now, the teacher remains the focal point of evaluating any educational system. For our ancestors, a teacher's qualifications varied depending upon the standards of the local community promulgated by its school board who were elected by the people. In very rural areas the qualifications were less demanding than in more urban areas, but many great teachers did not necessarily have the most education. They did, however, have a deep commitment to their students and they worked hard to give them the best education they could. The communities' teachers knew not only the students, but their parents and their brothers and sisters and their home environments. Many students came from the same family or were cousins or close relatives of the other students. As the teacher had taught these same family members for years, she or he knew which ones were good at math, reading or spelling and would call upon these older children to help the younger children learn. It was a very effective system. The teacher could select an older classmate who was admired and respected by the younger children to help. In a classroom of 30, the teacher might wisely use 10 or so older student "teachers" to help her. Both the older and younger student learned in the process. The older children learned by teaching and the younger child – delighted to get the attention of one of the older boys or girls – tried extra hard to learn from them. The system worked. Most of the children learned and grew up to be responsible adults pursuing their own dreams, maybe marrying and raising a family of their own and living near their parents or moving away to go to college and become artists, writers, doctors or preachers.

Colleges were established years ago by the wealthy and emperors and rulers but their purpose was not to teach their children how to make a living; their inheritances ensured that would not be necessary. Instead, parents wanted their children to learn how to learn, how to make intelligent decisions, how to think and solve problems, how to make good choices, how to be able to read and write and communicate orally and in writing in a persuasive and articulate fashion and how to appreciate their history and culture, its music, art and literature. In other words, college was a place to learn how to lead and try to leave the world a better place through their efforts. Ingrained in the system was a sense that an education carries a responsibility to help others.

In the final analysis, isn't that what a good education still means? Making a living is very important. It is essential that students learn to read, write and handle their financial affairs by learning math and other essential skills. But even if we could surgically implant a "smart chip" in every child's brain to enable them to read and write and recite their multiplication tables by heart, I am not sure we will have *educated* them until they grasp the importance of *why*. We've all seen it. Many "C" students or worse barely got through high school and some even college and then went to war or something happened in their lives that caused something to click: "Schooling is important." As a result they went back to high school or got their GED diploma or went to college or professional school and did very well. Why? Because they finally realized why they needed an education and were thankful for a second chance and did not waste it.

As we continue to emphasize the importance of our public education system, let us never forget the one-room schoolhouse and what it symbolizes. The most successful teachers believed in their students and encouraged them to believe in themselves. They also disciplined them as required and demanded respect, insisting on an atmosphere in which learning was not only possible but fun and rewarding. Both men and women – usually unmarried and often living with one of the parents of one or more of the students – were truly remarkable, dedicated individuals. Come to Heritage Farm and visit a one-room schoolhouse and six other museums to be reminded of the debt of gratitude we owe to these marvelous people, our ancestors, and the value they placed upon education and making sure that every child had an opportunity to get one.

THE LOG CHURCH

Collectively people spend millions of dollars each year in search of their genealogy or family tree, namely who were their ancestors and where did they come from. Many others, like the author, have not been very aggressive in this endeavor for fear of finding an incident in their family history involving a horse, a rope, a tree and people disputing the ownership of the horse. In all probability there would be a wide variety of people,  both good and bad, in most family trees. Look at the ancestors of Jesus. There were many good Kings and people anyone would have been proud to claim as part of their family. However, when you discover the bad Kings and the incestuous relationship between Judah and Tamar, as well as a former prostitute, Rahab, being an ancestor, as well as a relationship like David and Bathsheba which grew out of adultery and murder, we are assured that our genealogies are probably very much like others, a variety of both good and bad.

This is another way of saying that the people who crossed over the mountains into the rugged wilderness of Appalachia into what is today Southwest West Virginia and Eastern Kentucky were an equally complex group of people from all walks of life, good and bad, honest and dishonest, some with distinguished ancestors and others escaping from the law for perhaps not honoring their Indenture Commitment to work for someone for a number of years in exchange for paying for their boat passage to America or to avoid going to debtor's prison. Some may have distinguished backgrounds whose family had fallen on hard times or perhaps they were the younger brother who left the east coast when his older brother inherited everything or someone who left to marry the person whom their parents did not approve of. Most however were merely common people from various places in Europe. If we followed 100 men and women there would be 100 different stories as to why they were seeking a new beginning and crossing the mountains to find it.

The earliest settlers into Appalachia were neither all the drunken barbarians often depicted by some writers, nor were they all "Puritans" and people of impeccable character. There was a mixture. Each man and woman who crossed over the mountains also brought his or her own beliefs as to whether there was a God, and often even if they believed in a God, they did not believe he intervened in the affairs of men but only created everything, like a Clockmaker, and sat back and watched. They were called Deists and some of the founding fathers of our country held this belief. If you were a Deist, you did not believe in prayer as you believed God did not intervene in the affairs of people even if they asked him to. Of course there were also many people who did not believe in any God or divine creator.

These various beliefs and attitudes were very much influenced by events in their own lives, the beliefs and attitudes of their parents and from what part of the World they migrated to America from. The list of influencing factors is almost endless. However, once they settled down and started trying to build their own homes, clearing the land and preparing gardens and being totally responsible for finding and raising food to just feed themselves and their families and protecting them in the harsh wilderness in almost total isolation with perhaps your nearest neighbors being miles away, many people started rethinking their attitudes and religious beliefs.

Actually these changes may have started as they began crossing the mountains and walking thru vast forests of countless different varieties of trees, bushes, ferns, flowers and insects and hearing and seeing what must have seemed like hundreds of different birds and animals of all shapes and sizes and sleeping under a canopy of thousands of brilliant stars. Can you imagine the breathtaking sunrises and sunsets? Each new day brought new discoveries of a fabulous array of colors, greens, blues, browns, yellows, orange, etc., a true rainbow of beauty.

When they finally arrived at what would become their homestead they would further be reminded of what someone had taught them or they gradually learned themselves by trial and error that each tree was better suited for certain jobs than others; some were good for logs for their homes like poplar; cedar was good for shingles for their roofs; white oak for baskets, buckets and barrels; hickory for ax handles; pine for furniture and oak for beams. The same was true for their roots and leaves. Some were excellent as dyes to color their wool and others were wonderful medicines and tonics to cure illnesses.

They began to experience their dependency upon the weather -- the need for rain, but not too much or not too little, but just at the right time and in the right amount together with the right amount of sunshine. Wind could be a blessing and bring a cool breeze on a hot day but also unfortunately it could bring storms and devastation to their crops and even to the roofs of their homes. Our early settler's lives were governed by the weather, particularly the four seasons. There was a time to plow and plant, a time to hoe and to nurture the plants, a time to harvest, a time to preserve, a time to cut and store hay for the animals, a time to pick berries and a time to hunt, essentially a time for everything -- all governed by the unpredictable weather. Good weather meant plenty to eat and bad weather often meant almost starvation for everyone, both the people and their animals.

Are you beginning to see how perhaps their attitudes and religious beliefs began to change?

Remember the old adage "there are no atheists in foxholes". Perhaps some unbelievers who had never paid much attention to the weather and the infinite variety of nature gradually asked themselves where it came from and was it really possible that it just all happened without any purpose or design and most importantly, without a Creator?

Of course those early settlers who came into their new homes with long established religious beliefs only became more aware of the magnitude of their God and his creation and their worship and awe increased as well. Not worship in a formal church setting as we think of worship today but an active expression in the form of prayers and meditations, acknowledging the greatness of God and sensing his peace and comfort as they struggled with the hardships, trials and challenges of life, including illnesses, death and all the other inevitable aspects of life encountered by both believers and non-believers -- neither are spared. These believers would often find a special place and even a special time to be with the Lord. It might be on a mountain top, in a forest glen, beside a small stream or on a special rock. It might also be as they were going about their daily routines, plowing, cooking or tending the garden.

As people began to live closer together they might have started meeting together occasionally in each other's small log homes to worship. Maybe the peddler had told them about their various neighbors and which ones might wish to get together to worship. With the passage of time and the arrival of more people in the area, the believers would often gather together to build themselves a log church in which to engage in community worship. How happy they would be to now be able to sing and pray together and read from God's Holy Word, the Bible. Perhaps they took turns teaching and preaching or identified one of the groups to preach or bring a message of hope and encouragement. I doubt that denominational issues were important or that much time was spent debating religious issues or questions. One can imagine that with the passing of time this group of believers might be joined by some of the previous unbelievers. Their encounters with nature as well as observing how their "Church" neighbors dealt with the same adversities of life but with a greater sense of peace, hope and confidence, may have caused them to come to the little "Log Church" to see what was happening and discover the source of their hope and peace.

The log church at Heritage Farm Museum and Village outside of Huntington, WV is about 24 x 40 and holds about 80/100 people. It would have been very difficult for a few men to cut and hew, transport and erect logs of that weight and length without help. Accordingly an early log church would have been much smaller probably about half that length or about 20 x 20 which still would have taken considerable effort to build. As more and more people located in the area a larger log church like the one at Heritage Farm Museum and Village would have been built. In some communities it would have also served as the school and town hall as well as the church. It was truly the center of the community. Everyone wanted and preferred separate facilities but until the necessary time, resources and manpower were available they made do with what they had as best they could. How proud they were when they had three separate facilities. They must have felt they were on their way towards being a real town or village.

How sad it is today over a 100 years later to see some of these rural communities without their local schools, as they are consolidated in county wide schools and some even without many of their churches as they likewise have consolidated elsewhere due to declining and aging population. However, I am getting ahead of myself. Let's return to our early settlers in Appalachia.

We have probably all heard the old story that organized religion came to Appalachia in the following fashion—"The Baptists walked in-the Methodists rode in on their horses-the Presbyterians took the Stage Coaches and the Episcopalians traveled by train." Of course each religious group quarrels with who came first and how they traveled, but the story does illustrate how improved means of travel significantly changed the development of the Church and then Churches in an area. However, before means of travel, great religious revivals occurred in rural Appalachia, like Cane Brake Revival in Paris, Kentucky in 1801. It attracted an extremely large number of people and lasted a long time as people traveled considerable distances to be there. The author believes these revivals were extremely successful and that people were ready for a new way of life for the reasons discussed earlier, their dependency on nature and their encounters with their "Church" neighbors.

During this time the various circuit riders started to appear. These were preachers who rode their horses from community to community, preaching in the various churches, marrying couples, conducting funerals and otherwise pastoring the people. Somewhere along the line it happened. (The Baptist Church, The Methodist Church, The Presbyterian Church and so forth and so on and then came the 2nd Baptist Church or the Free Will Church of one denomination and then the others.) As the little communities grew, prospered and became towns and villages and some even cities, the churches grew with them. One can't help but wonder what caused all the divisions and whether more time and effort was now being spent arguing about religion and doctrine such as how often communion should be served and to whom and by whom-whether the pulpit should be in the center or on the left or right of it. The debates were and still are endless.

One can't help but wonder if the former non-believers in the communities were drawn to these various different churches they heard their "Church" neighbors arguing about, wondering who was right and who was wrong, which one was better than the other and whether the nature of the debates drew the non-believers to them in an effort to see what their "Church" neighbors had that they wanted. Even today is it the main line denominational churches that are growing or is it the community churches? One wonders how far we have fallen from the simple truth that "Jesus loves me this I know for the Bible tells me so" and that He loves our neighbors as well and that He wants us to love them the same way.

Maybe like the One Room School House, we fondly recall and still seek today the Simple Log Church where people of all ages, sizes and shapes were loved and nurtured by each other as they celebrated joys together as well as encouraged and nurtured each other in times of death, illnesses and other loses by worshipping their God in humble recognition that He created them for a purpose and equipped them to take care of His Creation and His people. Many of us are fortunate even today to be part of such a Godly community, whether part of a Denomination or not, and are blessed to still be singing about and praising and praying to the same Lord as our wonderful ancestors of years ago. Come and visit the Log Church at Heritage Farm and ring the church bell by pulling the rope as has been done for many generations and sit in one of the wood pews and seem to actually sense our religious forefathers and the sacrifices they made for us to insure that we have the privilege to continue to worship our God as we please. Let us never take these privileges and opportunities for granted but continue to attend worship services today in a church of our choice.

WORK

Our ancestors seemed more connected to each other, to the land and to their environment. Perhaps they had to be. Merely existing required many hands and lots of hard work to provide food from the land. Today, people are more removed and remote from their world and their relationship to the land and their environment. Even when we raise a vegetable garden or otherwise till the land for a beautiful flower garden or lawn, it is not vital to our existence. When we get tired, we can quit or if something else more interesting arises, we can readily shift our attention. We are not dependent upon what we grow. Life goes on regardless of the weather. Too much or too little sun or rain are inconveniences and even nuisances that often spoil our work or social activities, but we still eat and usually quite well.

I am becoming convinced that there was in the past more dignity in work, or perhaps it's more accurate to say there was a satisfaction in being more self-sufficient. Work has somehow become a bad word, or even worse, punishment. Too many people view work as something to be avoided and define success as not having to work. In reality work is a blessing and a meaningful part of life. Sadly, for many today, their work -- the means by which they earn their living -- is not very satisfying or fulfilling. They are happy to have a job but it is sometimes difficult to explain to their children what they do. It can be important and even necessary, but at the end of a long day, it is difficult to point to what you have done. Often what you have done only has to be done again and again the same way for long periods of time, almost endlessly. The nature of the industrial age – and now even the knowledge or information age – requires very different work patterns than experienced by our ancestors in the agriculture age. Much of their work was repetitious, like hoeing corn, but there was a clearer correlation between working and eating.

Many have lost the dignity of honest hard work, working with pride to accomplish a given task and the joy and satisfaction of a job well done when finished. When was the last time you dated something and signed or initialed it as your testament to the future of what you had done or accomplished?

Much of our work is certainly not glamorous and fulfilling, so it is even more important to find something to do in our spare time to do something satisfying. Make something. Grow something.

Maybe this is why many people like to mow their lawns after work. When finished, there is the satisfaction of pointing to the finished job and seeing tangibly what has been accomplished. Others can also see and enjoy what has been done.

Many employers and companies today are very large and it is easy for an employee to get lost and feel insignificant in the grand scheme of things. A lack of identity, in turn, can lead to struggles with self-esteem and value, even when the pay and benefits are above average. Our attitudes are extremely important toward overcoming this challenge. I'm reminded of the story of a newspaper reporter who was interviewing three workers at a job site, asking each one what he was doing. One answered, "Laying bricks." Another said, "Working on a wall." The third proudly announced, "I am building a church!" Attitude and perspective *are* important.

Much work in the past involved many members of the family. Some jobs, like harvesting, required everyone. Such work provided wonderful opportunities to develop good work ethics. You could learn to do your best, finish what you start and take pride in your work. Older members taught younger members the skills needed to provide for themselves and their families in the future. They also passed on the joys of life, like music, art, dancing and an appreciation of God's beautiful creation, including its ability to not only provide food, fruits and nuts, but plants and herbs with a wide variety of purposes, particularly medicinal. Parents did not rely upon the school or church to teach their children these vital life skills. Parents accepted that responsibility, realizing the consequences of their failure to do so. Imagine having to raise and provide your own food or to be your own doctor, nurse, dentist and veterinarian. Imagine having a sick child or spouse or a sick horse or cow vital for your survival and having to try to remember what to do by remembering what a parent or grandparent had tried to teach you.

Learning was essential to survival. Just as in the animal kingdom, parents had to teach their children how to care and provide for themselves and their families. Lessons not learned had painful – sometime fatal – consequences. However, children also observed the satisfaction and pride of a job well done by sharing in the labors of the family, each having a particular chore or task that was his or her responsibility and one the other members of the family depended upon. Maybe that is something we are missing, a feeling that everyone – regardless of age, size or even mental or physical infirmities – is needed and important. Even the smallest child helped. Everyone was loved but everyone was expected to contribute to the well-being of others, the family.

Maybe that is at least one explanation of one of our problems in today's society: too many people not working, expecting a free ride. Have we spoiled our children by not permitting them to learn the hard but important lessons we learned about work? In our effort to make life better for them, did we deprive our children of vital lessons and skills? Why did I not want my son to pass newspapers? I myself gained many important social insights concerning people by passing papers. I learned that the people in the big houses were not always the best "tippers" or even "payers." I learned not to judge the book by its cover. I also learned the discipline of having to get up early ever morning seven days a week, 365 days a year, and covering my route whether in the dark or rain or snow and collecting every week to pay for my papers. I learned that the difference between what I paid for the papers and what I collected plus any tips for great service (like putting the paper in a particular place as opposed to just throwing it) was mine to keep and spend as I chose. I learned the joy and satisfaction of saving my money and buying my first bicycle to help me pass my papers faster with less effort. On my paper route, I learned many lessons and values that served me well in life. So why did I not have my son do the same thing? Audy, of course, has done well in life, and apparently learned these values without passing papers. Maybe he was fortunate that we moved to a farm where he learned to feed and care for the animals that depended upon him. Actually, he learned these lessons working with his wonderful mother and his two sisters.

Nevertheless, why did I not have him pass papers? I think partially I was trying to allow him to have it "better" than I had it. I had worked hard and wanted him to enjoy some of the fruits of my labor. But I am not sure that completely or adequately explains my reluctance to have him pass papers or otherwise work to have spending money.

Could it have been my pride in not wanting my children to have to work to be more like their friends? Or did I subconsciously remember my father having to help me occasionally on a snowy Sunday morning when the papers were unusually heavy or needed extra protection to stay dry? As an aside, my lovely wife, Henriella, who worked hard all her life to provide herself her own spending money, made sure our children did not miss these experiences as they all worked at various and sundry odd jobs.

I am using myself as an example to show how easy it is to deprive our children of learning many invaluable lessons about work and self-reliance in a misguided attempt to give them something "better." In reality, we may be depriving them as we fail to teach them these essential skills they will need to provide for themselves and their families. The importance and dignity of work, the satisfaction of a job well done, the satisfaction of being independent and self-sufficient, of being able to dream big dreams and by means of hard work and determination, never quitting, make those dreams become a reality.

It is up to us as parents to teach our children the value of saving for rainy days and the uncertainties of life and growing old. It is up to us to teach them about how to handle their money and, when necessary, how to borrow it. We need to teach them it is not just how much down and how much a month. We need them to understand financial terms like "annual percentage rate" and "total finance charges," etc. We need to teach them to share and be concerned about others and their community. We need to teach them the importance of good health and taking care of themselves and their environment and to not be wasteful. We need to teach them to be thankful and to honor our God, the creator and sustainer of life to whom we all are and will be held accountable.

However, in the process of trying to provide for our families let us never forget the disastrous consequences of each generation not teaching its children how to care for themselves and their families by passing along to them these essential values, skills and attitudes vital for their ultimate happiness and well-being. These lessons are far more important than any amount of money or inheritance we could otherwise leave them. We cannot give this important responsibility to others like schools and churches. They can help but we cannot, and must not, shirk our own personal responsibilities. The well-being and happiness of our children and future generations depend upon us. Let us not fail them in this, one of our most important responsibilities as parents. Good luck.

TRANSPORTATION

Transportation is phenomenal today. People can travel and transport huge amounts of cargo thousands of miles around the world in hours, and that pales when compared to the speed and distances of travel in space. Of course, that has not always been the case and that story – the development of various means of transportation on land, water and in the air – is a wonderful way to teach history. It is a study perhaps more interesting than learning the names of presidents and wars and memorizing endless dates, which unfortunately was the way many of us were taught history in school. Actually the history of presidents, wars and dates is really the story of transportation and how it changed everything else, including presidents and wars.

Imagine a time when walking and running were the only way to cover distances on land or when swimming was the only way to move through water. And forget air travel for a long, long time. Now add the challenge of carrying any weight as you walked, ran or swam. People traveled relatively short distances and, for the most part, lived isolated from other people who lived even a relatively short distance away.

The development of the wheel and the cart and later the wagon, coupled with the domestication of animals, were huge steps forward in transportation on land as was the creation of rafts and canoes on water. For thousands of years, people traveled in basically the same way as did their parents and grandparents: walking, running, pulling a cart, riding an animal, or later, in a four-wheeled wagon being pulled by domesticated animals. Even on water, travel was limited to canoes and rafts until man was able to harness the wind and use sails to power his rafts and later his boats and ships at great lengths and much faster speeds. The world was beginning to change as was man as he learned to adapt to these new means of travel and transportation.

Whoever was able to move faster and quicker and carry heavier loads began to enjoy economic and military advantages over their slower neighbors. They prospered and began to explore and discover new and better foods. Unfortunately, they also learned how to subjugate and exploit other people with their newly discovered speed and strength. For example, remember Hannibal and his elephants, the Vikings with their ships and the Romans with their chariots?

History is not just the story of nations and their fates, but equally important, it is the story of the common man, the average person. People were able to migrate to new areas of their country and explore and occupy new lands. Such movements permitted more growth and less conflict over limited amounts of land and food. It also resulted in more subtle changes in the way people produced and purchased food and other products. There was now an advantage to produce more food and other products as it could be transported greater distances in less time, resulting in increased competition, which produced better prices and quality. As better means of transportation developed, a successful craftsman selling his wares – whether brooms, blacksmith items, furniture or cloth – had to produce better products than his competitor who was no longer in the same town or area. A boon to competition, improved transportation now permitted someone 50 and then 100 and then 150 miles away to transport their products and sell them farther distances from home.

These changes in transportation occurred over thousands of years, and in many respects, moved very slowly. Everything accelerated with the discovery of how to use steam to propel boats and then trains and even cars and trucks. Steam dramatically changed transportation and how people traveled, lived and worked and even where they lived and worked. This discovery occurred over a number of years but primarily happened in the early 1800s and continued into the 1900s.

Steam enabled boats to carry huge loads of cargo and people, not only with the current down rivers but also upstream against the current. No longer, for example in the United States where the products of Pittsburgh and Cincinnati were being sold in New Orleans and then around the world but now the products of the world and the South were able to be shipped up the Mississippi and Ohio to be sold along the river communities. Steamboats reigned supreme until the steam trains came along and eventually replaced them as a quicker and cheaper way to transport people and cargoes over longer distances, not just on rivers. However, steamships continued to be the ideal way to transport people and cargoes across the oceans and around the world. The world became smaller and smaller and nothing has ever been the same since the use of steam in transportation.

Not only did the steam train ultimately replace the steamboats, but the same thing happened to Conestoga wagons and stage coaches. With the new steam trains connecting the East Coast of America with the West Coast, the western migration of our great country got into high gear and has not slowed since. Not only were *people* moving to the Midwest and West, but so were products and manufactured goods, and later the goods of the West found their way to the East.

The steam trains not only replaced the steamboats but signaled the end of many canals across the nation which had been built to enable towns and communities not located on rivers to compete with those that did. Canals were built across states like Ohio from the Great Lakes to the Ohio River and boats were pulled by horses and mules along the canals, but they could not compete with steam trains for speed or ability to carry extremely heavy loads for less money.

Roads were not very good and much fewer than today, but there were steam-powered cars available which traveled at very fast speeds, far surpassing a good horse and buggy. For many years steam-powered boats, trains, ships and automobiles ruled supreme in the world of transportation and greatly impacted the lives of every person in America. Steam was a major influence in driving what we today call the "Industrial Age of

America." People began to work in factories instead of living on farms raising food. It took thousands and perhaps even millions of workers to build these boats and trains as well as to dig the coal and iron ore, make the steel, dig the tunnels, build the bridges, lay the track for the trains and build the roads and bridges for the automobiles. These new industries needed capitalists, engineers and hundreds of new types of support groups to enable them to develop and expand across this great nation.

What happened next and why are we not still traveling by steam? But wait a minute -- we still use steam to travel. Where do you think most of our electricity comes from? Steam. We burn coal, gas and even nuclear fuel to heat water into steam to turn turbines to generate electricity. Probably close to 80 percent of our electricity today comes from steam -- basically everything but wind, solar and hydro.

But what happened to steam-powered transportation? The ingenuity and creativity of man and the developments of science and technology produced internal combustion engines fueled by gasoline and diesel. These motors and diesel-powered trains replaced steam-operated ones and diesel-powered ships displaced the steam ones and the gas-powered cars surpassed the steam and electric cars.

What? Wait a minute – electric cars? Did you think hybrid and electric cars were today's new technology? Actually, no. Electric cars and trucks have been around for more than 100 years. In fact, there is a 1908 electric truck in the Transportation Museum at Heritage Farm Museum & Village. There were many electric vehicles at the turn of the century and probably steam and electric automobiles outnumbered the combustion vehicles. An interesting story to pursue on another occasion is why the gas-powered cars replaced the electric and steam vehicles. Along that line, did you know that there has been over 2,600 different companies manufacturing automobiles, not just models, in the United States? How many are left today? Come to Heritage Farm and see the list and see if someone with your last name or your mother's maiden name ever manufactured a car, and if so, how long did it last?

There really is no end to the story of transportation. We have not even mentioned the unicycle, high-wheeler, bicycle, motorcycle, hot air balloon, glider and dirigible. We will leave those subjects to others, but can't omit further mention of the automobile, particularly Henry Ford's Model T and the Wright brothers' airplane. Like steam, these gentlemen took changes in transportation to a new level. Although Mr. Ford did not invent the automobile, his innovations in mass production and the use of assembly lines to produce 15 million Model T's at an inexpensive price, at times under $400, to the masses, as opposed to the previous hand-crafted automobiles which were sold for thousands of dollars to the wealthy. As a result, Mr. Ford went a long way towards establishing the middle class in America. They were often the people who worked in his factories and made enough money at $5 a day to buy a Model T themselves. Mr. Ford was reputed to have asked people who tried to sell him robots or automatic welding devices, "How many Model T's will your machine buy?" The competition between Ford and Chevrolet -- which continues today -- spelled the end of the Model T in 1928 and caused him to come out with his Model A, of which he also sold 15 million. These numbers are staggering and demonstrate how widespread and popular the automobile became. It was no longer a luxury. It became a necessity and again our world has not been the same since.

At almost the same time the automobile industry was beginning, the Wright brothers, Orville and Wilbur, from Dayton, Ohio, invented the airplane in the early 1900s. This began a process that has greatly expanded the speed and distances people and cargoes could be transported around the world and led to developments that enable man to explore space at unbelievable speeds. Air travel has caused us to live in a "global economy" today where businesses, workers and craftsmen have to compete with their counterparts all over the world, i.e., China, India, etc., as goods and products can travel around the world in less than a day.

This global competition has also been greatly affected by developments in transportation on water, particularly the oceans of the world. Huge cargo vessels carrying oil and other vitally needed products and raw materials, as well as extremely large liners carrying thousands of people, have truly shrunk the world and opened up new vistas in travel and competition all over the world. Nuclear-powered submarines can now travel under the seas for very long periods of time in yet another example of change in transportation never envisioned by our ancestors, who also could never have imagined space travel.

None of us can imagine how transportation will continue to change on land, on and under water as well as in the air, including outer space. However, change it will. Our study of the past, our history, shows us the almost inextricable inevitability of change -- something new and better, with its attendant challenges to our economies and environment. There will be winners and losers as there have been winners and losers in the past as each new development in transportation occurred. Remember, it is not necessarily who invents something but who can figure out how to use it in a manner people are willing to buy with their hard-earned money. Don't forget the automobile was not invented in the United States, nor did we first discover how to harness the power of steam or invent the external combustion engine. However, we were able to use these inventions in a dramatic way to change the lives of average people, not just the rich or the emperors as in most countries. Let us not ever forget our history and forfeit our ability to help the common man, that mythical average person, to live a richer, fuller and more meaningful life by harnessing new energies and new "power sources" as they are discovered for the betterment of us all and our World.

At Heritage Farm Museum & Village, visit the Transportation Museum, one of six different museums at the Farm depicting the story of our ingenious and creative ancestors and how their hard work and determination has truly changed our world and the way we live, work and play. Enjoy seeing the horse-drawn carriages and wagons of our past, particularly a Contestoga wagon and a Wells Fargo stage coach. Examine a 1908 electric truck with 42 batteries which was used to deliver the Saturday Evening Post in Philadelphia. See a 1910 Sears automobile and discuss why Sears did not dominate the automobile industry with its widespread catalog, distribution system and immense capital. Learn how the Model T was made as well as viewing a number of Model T's and A's. Experience model exhibits demonstrating the importance of steam as well as the development of trains and steamboats. Don't forget the airplane suspended from the ceiling. "By experiencing the past we can learn to appreciate the present, today, and dream about a better tomorrow, the future." Come for an hour or a day or spend a week in one of the beautiful log homes located there. Learn why it is said that the past, our history, provides a wonderful window to our future.

PROGRESS

One of the best ways to appreciate how different our lives are from that of our ancestors is to consider how everyday activities – and even the basic ways we provide food and clothing for ourselves – have changed over the years. Along the way, we will also learn a little more about where we have come from and how we got here.

Learning history this way is not the study of presidents and wars and memorizing dates as we often did in school, but rather is learning history from observing the daily routines of ordinary people. This is how you learn the basics, like building and furnishing homes, raising and providing food, cooking and preserving it, making cloth and clothes and washing and ironing them, personal hygiene and even entertaining ourselves. These routines have changed over the years, some gradually, some dramatically, and studying these changes can help us prepare for the future and even create a brighter future.

Man's earliest years were nomadic. People roamed the land, living in caves and then tents, searching for food that was eaten raw and later cooked over an open fire. Gradually, some people started settling in a particular location, usually preferring to live near water, and they began to cultivate their own food -- by both farming and continuing to hunt and fish. They began to build more permanent homes and cook food inside their homes but still on open fires. With few tools and instruments or even pots and pans, nothing changed significantly in that primitive life for thousands of years.

Gradually – with the discovery of ways to refine metal, make pottery and then glass and how to domesticate animals – the world began to change in ways that would be recognizable to America's earliest settlers as well as to the first settlers who came later to the mountains of Appalachia.

Lives of the people who settled along the Atlantic Ocean began to improve as transportation improved from England and Europe and their early industrial society started providing better products to deliver to America. Early settlers gradually began to live in towns and villages, no longer in cabins and forts but in wood and brick homes, with an increasing variety of craftsmen to provide them with not only the necessities of life but many were now able to purchase "luxuries" and the other fine things available in other parts of the world.

The history of a people often is presented as a single story, but of course, that story differs greatly depending on where your subject lived and how much money he or she had to spend. In other words, the history of Boston or Philadelphia in 1750 or 1800 is quite different from that of life in rural southwest

Virginia or Eastern Kentucky at the same time. In fact, even regions of the same state have different stories to tell; the history of an old city like Wheeling or the relatively affluent Eastern Panhandle of what is today West Virginia was also quite different from the rural southwest sections.

Still, generally speaking, the lives and daily activities of the early settlers who came across the mountains from the East were not that much different from the early settlers to America. Their housing, the way they cooked and made their clothing and footwear, preserved their food or otherwise went about their daily routines to survive were not that different. If they were fortunate, their firearms and a few pots and pans might have improved a little but basically things were about the same. The early trapper and explorer lived in a cave or a log lean-to and later perhaps a tent. He cooked over an open fire, much the same way as his ancestors thousands of years before him. He started fires the same way -- with flint. His clothing and footwear had not changed much and were usually made out of animal pelts and skins. His firearms were better than clubs, bows and arrows but tremendous skill was still required to hunt and trap and survive against the elements in a hostile environment.

Things improved slightly as the trapper or explorer brought his wife and family over the mountains to join him. They built log cabins with chimneys to heat themselves in the winters and in which to cook their food -- inside but still on an open fire. By hand, they cleared the land of trees with axes and planted gardens to raise food for themselves. They were often able to carry very little with them as they primarily walked over the mountains accompanied at best by a horse and later perhaps a cow, a pig, a dog, a sheep or goat or perhaps some chickens. These few animals and their family had to be protected from a wide variety of wild animals in the wilderness. If they wanted something they had not brought with them, they had to make it or learn to do without.

Back across the mountains on the East Coast were many artisans and craftsmen – furniture makers, weavers, spinners, coopers, tinsmiths, blacksmiths and candle makers – who could make many labor-saving devices, from churns and buckets to grist mills and saw mills. The East even had stores to sell these products and other goods from around the world. On the western side of the mountains, furniture, churns, tubs, buckets, apple peelers, juicers, spinning wheels, looms, brooms and more had to be handmade. On the East Coast, if you wanted a wool coat, you went to a farmer and got some wool and then you went to the carding mill and then to the spinner and then to the dyer to get the right color. Next, you took these items to the weaver and then to the tailor or seamstress. You were also able to purchase buttons and decorative furs. Not so for the lady on the other side of the mountains in Appalachia. She had to do all these tasks herself to get a coat and could not stop all her other arduous chores like cooking, tending the garden, caring for the children and animals, washing, etc.

As transportation improved – first with better roads and canals, then the development of steamboats in the early 1800s, ultimately steam trains which replaced them – not only did this change life on the East Coast, but it also altered life everywhere in America. Trains first connected the West Coast to the East Coast, but then gradually they began to come to more remote portions of Appalachia. The goal was often to provide access to the timber, coal, oil and other products needed for the industrial growth of America. Appalachia's natural resources were the fuel for the production of steel necessary to build the trains, automobiles and skyscrapers rapidly changing the landscape of our country. And that also fueled the growth of the region. For example, when West Virginia became a state in 1863, it had fewer than 400,000 people; before 1900, it had grown to more than a million people, many of them new immigrants who had come to America to find work building the railroads, then stayed to cut the timber and mine the coal.

Appalachia was forever changed. More and more people moved to the cities where factories were being built to manufacture a wide variety of products, all using an abundance of raw materials, including water, oil, gas and coal. Even in rural areas there were country stores. In mining communities, this was called the company store, where you could buy clothes and shoes, food, hardware, almost anything you would want if you could pay for it.

As the Industrial Revolution rolled on, fewer people across the nation were making things for themselves; instead, they were working in factories and spending their wages to buy things – cast iron stoves, ice boxes, treadle sewing machines, furniture, hardware and medicines – that other people made in other factories.

In Appalachia, people continued to cling to their life patterns and raised gardens, canned, made quilts, picked berries, made and played musical instruments and hunted and fished as their world changed around them. Large cities had electricity, indoor plumbing and other more modern conveniences not yet available in rural areas. A kitchen in the southern rural part of West Virginia in the early 1900s had come a long way from the kitchen of the early settler. Even without electricity you had kerosene lamps instead of candles, cast iron cook stoves instead of cooking on an open hearth, you might have a wooden washing machine instead of a scrub board and maybe a Singer treadle sewing machine instead of just a needle and thread to hand sew with. What a luxury it must have seemed to be able to hand pump water in the kitchen without having to carry it from the well or creek. Wagons and buggies were great advances in local transportation as was the iron plow, harrow and planters in farming. In some of the larger areas, even the telephone was beginning to become available if they could find enough subscribers willing to pay for it.

One of the greatest changes was the availability of the Sears Roebuck catalog. Now the products of the world were available even in rural areas. There's nothing better than the catalogs to illustrate the magnitude of the changes between the middle of the 1800s and the early 1900s. When people are asked why there was not a Sears catalog in 1850, the usual answer is that the company had not yet been formed. That is true, of course. But why had Sears not been started? And what would have happened if it had? Failure. In 1850, you could not have printed and distributed a free catalog. A visit to the printing exhibit in the Progress Museum at Heritage Farm will show you that at that time, printing was still primarily being done by setting type by hand, one laborious letter at a time, and the printing was being done one page at a time. Pictures would have been very expensive and the catalog would have cost a fortune. How would you have delivered it to rural areas without a dependable mail service? How would you have placed your order, and perhaps most important, how would you have delivered a heavy cast iron stove from Chicago to rural Appalachia without steam trains? There also would not have been as many manufactured products and goods to sell in 1850.

Life in rural Appalachia started making more significant changes in the 1920s and '30s with the availability of electricity. Natural gas had been available in some areas and was used for heating, cooking and lighting. Large batteries and even generators on windmills had been used to generate electricity but real progress began when electrical systems and lines were installed at least in more populated areas. (But even in the 1950s, I had classmates who still did not have electricity or indoor plumbing because of the remote location of their homes.) Talk about taking things for granted! We were children with and without these conveniences going to the same school.

Change did not come easily for some, and it could be frightening. The competition between gas and electricity was fierce. The electric company said gas blew people up; the gas company said electric burned you up or electrocuted you. The publicity fed fears and made it that much more difficult to get some people to adapt to new ideas. But for those who did, there were great rewards. Imagine having a refrigerator instead of an ice box, an electric washing machine instead of a wooden hand washer. Now you could get electric lights instead of gas or kerosene as well as electric toasters, mixers, churns, ice cream makers, fans, sweepers, irons and clocks. What wonders! New affordable automobiles like Mr. Ford's Model T were available for less than $400, though, of course, that was still a lot of money if you only made $2 a day. But now there were jobs that paid $4 or $5 a day. There was a dependable mail service and in some areas, if you were fortunate, you could even get a private telephone line as opposed to the previous party line which had enabled neighbors to listen in on other people's conversations.

And then there was radio. Now people in rural areas could keep abreast of what was happening around the world as well as be entertained. People gathered around the radio and watched it as they listened to such great programs like "Lum and Abner," "Amos and Andy," and "Fibber McGee and Molly." They used their imagination to create vivid pictures of what their favorite characters were doing. In fact, older people often say that not even television or the special effects of Hollywood are as good as the images they created in their minds while listening to the old radio programs.

Curiously, in many respects, particularly in the kitchen, things have not changed much since then. Other than the microwave, there are not that many new appliances that our mothers and grandmothers did not have in the 1920s and '30s. Henriella and I discovered this when after antique collecting for many years and furnishing three kitchen exhibits in the Progress Museum -- including one in a log cabin around 1850, the second around 1900 and the third around 1925. We began searching for items for a kitchen from the 1950s and later. Although the later kitchens looked different, we discovered that basically the appliances and devices had not changed that much. We still use gas and electricity, the washing machine either has an agitator or drum as it has had for over 100 years and the mixer had more speeds. So, instead of showing various other kitchens since 1925, we display a wide variety of cook stoves, washers, sweepers, irons and other household devices to demonstrate how things have continued to change as progress marches on.

That observation about kitchen appliances caused me to reflect upon the magnitude of change since the advent of electricity. Of course, we now have television and computers as well as wireless telephones and countless other electronic devices that keep getting more powerful and smaller each year, but the question remains: what's next? Is there more to come? It has been said that someone -- when asked to head the U.S. Patent Office around the late 1800s or early 1900s -- questioned whether there was anything else worthwhile to be invented. In his mind, there was no need to keep the Patent Office open. Progress was over. We often think the same way and have difficulty imaging a future different from the present.

But that is one of the best reasons to study history. Our past gives us a wonderful doorway into the future. What resident of a log cabin in rural Appalachia in the mid-1800s could have ever imagined flying in a plane or driving a car or having electric lights as well as air conditioning, heat and indoor plumbing? However, it happened. The candle gave way to whale oil which was replaced by kerosene lights which were surpassed by gas and electric lights. Sewing by hand became the treadle sewing machine and then the electric sewing machine to a time when most people no longer sew.

We hope a visit to the Progress Building at Heritage Farm will cause you to imagine a different future -- not just new gadgets, but new sources of energy and power, causing the rebuilding and retooling of America and the world. Today's computers are marvelous but their importance will pale when compared to the discovery of new energy sources and powers. Right now some bright mind is perhaps working on this possible discovery and when it happens, that individual or group of individuals will make so much money that they will make Bill Gates look like a pauper. Just remember the changes in our history caused by new energy sources like water, wind, steams, electricity and nuclear and imagine what lies ahead in a brighter and cleaner future powered in a manner none of us can yet imagine.

LEGACY

Did you receive a legacy? Was it from your parents or others? What was it? What, if any, is the legacy you are leaving to others?

Your legacy is not limited to what you legally inherited from your parents or other ancestors, but often

 far more important, it is the lessons and values you learned and otherwise received from them. Things like a good name, character developed by whatever type of discipline required, a strong work ethic and other intangible values and principals gained as a part of life experiences. Those lessons often included for many of us things like:

-- Do your best.

-- Be a person of honor and integrity, someone others trust and respect, because you are a person of your word, a person whose word is his or her bond and a person who does what he or she promises.

-- Learn how to get along, respect others and not to think too highly of yourself.

-- Learn from your mistakes and try not to make the same ones twice, but remember it is better to try and fail if you did your best rather than not try at all because you can always try again and often, through persistence and learning from your mistakes, ultimately succeed.

-- Learn the dignity of work, including hard manual labor, and the magnificent gift of a good night's sleep from being tired, yet with a satisfying feeling of accomplishment.

-- Waste not, want not.

-- Play by the rules and clean up your own messes.

-- Save and plan for the future; don't just live for today.

-- Realize you can learn something from almost everyone, particularly those who did not go to college, who can often do many things that those who did can't.

-- Be generous by sharing and helping others.

-- Respect yourself and don't abuse your body or mind.

-- And, be proud of your heritage, your community, your state and your country.

The list is endless and each person's list is somewhat different. However expressed, your legacy defines who you are and who you are becoming.

At times, it seems like everything I have needed to know in life I now realize I learned at home, grade school and Sunday school. Not that I did not learn a great deal in high school, college and professional school. What I learned in high school, college and professional school enabled me to earn a good living and support my family, which is very important. However, enjoying life and living it with a sense of purpose and meaning and gaining a sense of well-being and satisfaction which leads to true happiness, joy and contentment mostly comes from the lessons I learned early in life and tried to adhere to throughout the balance of my life. Those lessons are those I discussed above, my legacy, from my family, friends, public and Sunday school teachers, coaches, Scout leaders, neighbors and all those countless other people who gave of themselves by influencing me in both positive and negative ways. From some, those I admired, I learned what I wanted to be, and from the others, how I did not want to be.

I was indeed fortunate to grow up during a time when, not only at home and Sunday school, but at public school as well, from wonderful teachers I respected and trusted, I learned that God created man, including me, with a purpose and that He loved me and everyone in the world and that He wanted us to honor Him by the way we treated other people. We were taught that God wanted us to love Him with all of our heart, soul, strength and mind and to love our neighbor as ourselves. We learned to respect our parents and not talk back to them, particularly our mothers -- which was an extremely serious offense instantly punished by our fathers. We learned to respect our elders and to treat other people the way we would want them to treat us. We learned to salute the flag and say the Pledge of Allegiance and -- more important -- to read from the

Bible, God's Holy Word, because it gave us the basics to build a good life upon. We were taught to appreciate God's incredible creation and to care for it and ourselves by eating properly and getting plenty of good exercise. We were taught to leave things better than we found them and to try to make the world a better place, starting with our own homes and communities. However, more than anything else, I have become convinced, as I have gotten older and observed the unexplainable mysteries of life, that your legacy is that uniqueness given to you by your Creator, and as someone said:

"Who you are is God's gift to you -- who you become is your gift to God."

If you were as fortunate as I to learn these lessons growing up, we both are exceedingly rich and that is our real legacy, not any monetary inheritance. If those early lessons are truly learned in childhood and faithfully obeyed throughout life, they are far more valuable than silver and gold and will bring you more happiness, joy and contentment -- things money can't buy. Don't get me wrong -- having money is not in itself bad; it can be wonderful. However, if focusing on accumulating only money at the expense of loss of character, integrity and morality, then that is a price too dear and far too expensive. Money alone does not guarantee those attributes that give life meaning and purpose, peace of mind and a sense of well-being and satisfaction.

Our legacy – our values, roots, heritage, culture, whatever and however you describe it – was passed on from generation to generation more often than not during conversations often while working. That's when it was explained to us why it was important for us to do our best and to do whatever we promised to do. It may have involved a mother or a grandmother teaching a daughter how to quilt and answering questions as to why the stitches needed to be so small or where the material came from. Grandmother would then remember what her mother or grandmother told her while she was learning to sew, cook, weave, or whatever, about pride in your work and satisfaction of a job well done. Fathers, grandfathers and others passed along similar values and lessons to sons and grandsons while hunting, fishing or working together. Conversation naturally flowed about the past and the hardships they endured and the difficulties they overcame, but always with the appreciation of the blessings they had received and the joys of life, never taking anything for granted. Often these same values and lessons were passed on by observing our loved ones and others as they went about doing the various chores and tasks of life, putting a roof over our heads and putting food on the table or watching them doing their work with great pride and satisfaction.

My purpose in writing this is to remind ourselves of the importance of finding or making time to spend with our family, as well as with other children and young people to pass on to them the important lessons of life we have learned. Remember, this does not occur successfully as lectures, but in informal settings, usually while people are otherwise enjoying themselves. The wisdom of experience or inexperience is wasted if not passed on. The listeners may choose to ignore our counsel, perhaps as we ourselves did to our detriment, but our responsibility is to try.

Perhaps there are not as many of these teachable moments available to us today for a variety of reasons.

Often we are not involved in making or repairing things around the house. We either hire someone to do such things or, more often than not, throw old or broken things away or buy something new to replace it. Family members are often also involved in their own activities which unfortunately usually revolve around various electronic devices, like television, computers, video games -- the list goes on and on. Life is often quite structured with lessons, organized sports and other activities leaving families little time to talk with each other even at meals together. Between work and our normal routines, there is little free time to enjoy each other let alone find time to teach things we hope or assume are being taught at school or church.

If you need help creating such opportunities, let me suggest a visit to Heritage Farm Museum & Village with your family or church group. Stay overnight in one of the homes that helps create the right atmosphere, yet with all the modern conveniences, other than TV, and take a tour of the various museums. In a setting focused on our rich heritage, one quickly sees how our lives today are significantly different than in years gone by. Notice I said different, not necessarily better. In most respects, things are better. The advances in medicine, transportation and communication are truly phenomenal, not to forget the modern conveniences of electricity, indoor plumbing, central heating and air conditioning, etc. The list of advancements in providing us a greatly enhanced quality of life is almost endless.

However, the question remains: Have we lost anything in the process and, if so, what and how can we regain it?

I believe the answer is yes. The answer is hard to explain, but do we believe that people are happier and more satisfied today with who they are and what they are doing and accomplishing with their lives? Are they more content? I am not arguing for us to return to the so called "Good Old Days," but I am trying to raise the question as to whether we can take advantage of all of our modern conveniences without giving up some of the best characteristics of our ancestors. Can we regain that sense of self-sufficiency and enhanced self-esteem? Can we have that sense of purpose and fulfillment in life that gives it dignity and meaning? The answer is clearly yes. We must!

Please spend some time reflecting upon the people who positively and negatively influenced your life and helped make you who you are today, and even more important, who you want to become in the future. Remember and think about the values and lessons you were taught, your legacy. Then add to that legacy the additional lessons you have learned the hard way throughout your life and commit to pass that legacy on to the next generation. Make the time and create the opportunities to pass that legacy on to, not only your family, but make an effort to share it with other children and young people who are not fortunate enough to have someone in their lives to share with and teach them.

The values and lessons of the past -- our legacy -- are lost if not passed on from generation to generation. It only takes a break of one link in the chain of history to disconnect the future from the past. The past is often described as a doorway to the future and it is important that we preserve the best aspects of our rich heritage -- our past -- and work hard to pass these values and lessons onto our children and grandchildren to remind them as well as ourselves how much we take for granted the wonderful quality of life we enjoy today and realize how much better the future can be if we can combine the best of the present with the values and lessons we learn from our past.

NOSTALGIA

What is the fascination with the past?

I began this section of the book with a discussion about people yearning for "The Good Old Days," and it seems appropriate to wrap up with some thoughts on why some think life in yesteryear was simpler and that the families there were closer.

Why *did* our grandparents and earlier ancestors seem happier and more content with life, even though they lacked all the modern conveniences we take for granted today? What *is* it that we feel we are missing that we believe they possessed?

The question may be stated many different ways. In fact, in many instances the question can't even be precisely phrased, but is reflected by the gnawing feeling by many that we are lacking something that many people in the past seemed to enjoy and that something, whatever it is, has been lost.

The answer remains somewhat illusive. What could possibly be attractive about living without indoor plumbing, electricity, central heat and air conditioning? Who really wants to go back to the horse and buggy for transportation or the pony express or the telegraph for communication? Who would want to not have available all the modern life-saving medicines and hospitals, as well as professional trained doctors and nurses to care for us? Who would really want to return to having their babies in their homes with no one to help other than family or perhaps a midwife?

There are a few brave souls who are willing to forego these modern conveniences for various reasons but not many, and certainly not myself. Yet we continue to feel we are missing something. What is our fascination with the Amish or visiting and studying the various communal groups of the past like the Shakers? It is a challenge to try to define what we believe we are missing or have lost, and whether we can regain it without sacrificing our modern conveniences.

Do we really believe people in the past were more honest? Do we really want to return to the glory days of the Old West and Wyatt Earp and Marshall Dillon? Hasn't crime, even murder, been with us since the beginning with Cain slaying Abel? Drunkenness, stealing, cheating and fraud are nothing new. I am reminded of this every time I pick up the Auto Theft Device manufactured in 1914 to prevent people from stealing cars. It probably isn't a belief that people were somehow more honest in days gone by that is the answer to our quest.

Did everyone work to support themselves and families? Did husbands and even wives ever leave home and abandon their children? Were all businessmen and politicians honest? Was life really better working 10 to 12 hours a day? Did everyone go to church? Was everyone really happy? The answers to these questions are obvious, yet we continue to believe something is missing.

Was life really simpler? If simplicity is the absence of choices, it might have been. For most people in a rural agricultural society life, each day was focused on providing food, clothing and shelter and tending to the animals and land that were essential to survival. In addition to one's own work, life on the farm was very much influenced by the weather and forces completely beyond the farmer's control, like having the right amount of sun and rain, not too much and not too little. Everyone in the family had responsibilities and chores and had to work together to provide life's necessities. It was anything but easy. Life was hard. Anyone who has hoed corn, put up hay, dug potatoes, or picked beans can attest to that. It was satisfying, but still hard work often in the hot sun in the heat of the day. However, worse than the hard work was the uncertainty of whether your crops would grow and survive due to bad weather, raids by animals or fire. Does not sound easy or simple to me.

Nevertheless, the yearning persists. I am not sure we know the answer, and if the answer were found, it would probably be different for each person. Still, let me offer perhaps part of the answer, at least for me.

Our life today is extremely complex for most of us. We are surrounded by things we do not understand, can't make or even repair. This is, unfortunately, not only true in our homes but at our places of employment as well. Electronic gadgets and computers baffle most of us -- not how to use them, but how they work. In fact, many older people like me have to wait for one of our grandchildren to show us how to use these devices. When is the last time you tried to repair something? A few people are able to do so but the vast majority of us are lost. We have become a "throw away society." New and improved products are introduced so often that parts of old products are no longer available or cost more than the new item itself. Even if you used to enjoy tinkering with "tuning up your old car engine," today you are lucky to find the spark plugs, and if you find them, you probably don't have the special wrenches needed to remove them.

Perhaps this is why we admire the artifacts of the past. They were often handmade with great pride and satisfaction with dates and names or initials on them as reminders to the future that they existed. Who can resist the beauty and creativity of a hand-stitched quilt made with recycled clothing or the smooth comfortable handmade tools of the craftsman of yesteryear? Who has not been amazed at the infinite variety of almost every product or device these people constantly made to make their lives a little better?

Those people understood their world. They made their own devices to reduce their work load or improve their productivity. They were able to provide for themselves. Imagine being able to build your own home, raise and produce your own food and even make your own clothing and footwear. They knew the satisfaction of a job well done and had pride in their work. They experienced joy and satisfaction in providing life's necessities for themselves and their families. They knew contentment at the end of the day and the joy of a good night's sleep, tired from hard work, but having the satisfaction of having done their best and surrounded by their loved ones who shared that love.

Things seem to control us today instead of us controlling things. In fact, it may be even worse than that for many. The more things we have, the more things we believe we need. Life seems almost defined by our accumulation of things. We somehow believe our ancestors learned to be content with what they had or at least what they reasonably could expect to get. We are fascinated by the stories of our elders, particularly at Christmas, when they tell us of the joy of receiving an orange or a handmade toy. We compare this to our experiences of hearing children ask us "Is that all?" after they had spent at least an hour in non-stop opening of expensive gifts. Don't get me wrong, we adults are every bit as bad as our children.

Maybe we have too much time on our hands. Old-timers often said, "Idle hands were the Devil's handiwork." How many times have you heard children complain there is nothing to do or adults echoing similar thoughts? Even when we have spare time, we have difficulty using it wisely. How often have you heard there is nothing worth watching on TV? However, we continue to sit there and watch TV. These spare moments were few and far between in the past, but when they did occur, they were used to make something -- a quilt or a musical instrument. Can you imagine making a banjo or fiddle and teaching yourself how to play it and then later teaching someone else how to play it or make one as well? Crafts and skills were preserved and passed on from generation to generation. Thankfully, there are people today who use their time wisely and can make many wonderful objects with their own hands, just not as many.

At Heritage Farm Museum & Village, we have worked for many years to collect, preserve and display in educational venues our rich Appalachian heritage and culture. Come and experience life as it was and see how our ancestors ingeniously created a much improved world for us. Learn why it is said that the past is truly the doorway to the future. Slow down and spend some time with your family reconnecting with the best of our rich legacy, our heritage and culture. Recommit yourself to not taking people and things for granted and perhaps reorienting your time and priorities. Turn off all the electronic gadgets and enjoy talking or playing games with each other or perhaps just work a puzzle. You might even want to sign up for courses to learn how to sew by hand or on a treadle sewing machine like your grandmother used, or quilt, weave, spin, braid rugs, etc. You might want to learn to work with wood or iron or just walk and hike and otherwise enjoy God's beautiful creation on our 500 acres with miles of trails. Learn to better appreciate what we take for granted today, a fabulous quality of life that can be improved and enjoyed by not forgetting our rich heritage and perhaps learning to do something productive ourselves with our own hands and developing our own sense of creativity, beauty and pride while at the same time also learning to be more thankful for what we do have and spend less time and emotional energy worrying about what we do not have.

CONCLUSION
BY MIKE PERRY

People come to the museum at Heritage Farm Museum & Village for so many different reasons.

Some want to reminisce about the past, recalling their own youth or reliving the times they've imagined from the stories of their parents or grandparents. Others yearn for the "Good Old Days," a time they mistakenly suppose was a slower, calmer way of life. Funny how they think our forefathers somehow enjoyed a simpler, happier existence having been spared the frustrations and anxieties of our own time. For other guests, it's a sense of history that compels them, a thirst for knowledge and understanding, or just plain and wonderful curiosity! Almost all of them want to be entertained, to seek adventure in the unknown.

What we hope for our guests is that they come with an anticipation of learning something that will benefit them sometime in the future. That's why Heritage Farm's motto is "Study the past to gain an appreciation of the present and dream and plan for the future."

But how could looking at a collection of tools and accessories of yesteryear help us today or in the future? What lessons could we as individuals or companies learn from the past?

Such lessons are what history does best. Consider that more than 2,600 different companies have made automobiles in the United States since 1900, and that only two or three of those companies are left. Or consider that countless numbers of washing machine manufacturers have existed in the same period, and yet very few have survived to today. What can we learn from determining what they did right and what they did wrong? Why did some survive and most fail? Do these lessons apply only to companies or do they have messages for individuals, families and other organizations as well?

Change, as I've noted throughout this book, fascinates us here at Heritage Farm. We believe these examples from the past teach us the importance of adapting, and of learning to deal with all types of change. Repeatedly, history shows us that those who adapted to changes – in methods of transportation and communication and other technological changes – are the ones who survived. A few even prospered. And those who did not adapt failed and ultimately went out of business. In one of the reflections in the previous section, we cited the printing business as a prime example. Imagine being an expert typesetter, perhaps one of the fastest in the trade. For a time, you command an excellent wage and can find work anywhere you travel. But how dramatically your world would change around 1900 with the arrival of the Linotype machine. That one innovation enabled a single operator to outproduce four or five typesetters like you. And now, ask yourself how many Linotype operators do you know today? Sadly for them, advances in technology replaced the Linotype operators the same way that they had replaced the typesetters. And, as we noted, unfortunate consequences for *them* proved very fortunate for the rest of us. We greatly benefited by having more books, more newspapers and more magazines available at significantly lower prices. A big lesson of history and a centerpiece of many of our exhibits is that progress usually comes at the expense to some and the benefit to others. And it is an ongoing story. Changes in the world today in how goods are manufactured and shipped are only a part of a long history of similar changes. How people and companies successfully and unsuccessfully have dealt with those changes makes all the difference. At Heritage Farm, we believe the lessons we can learn from the mistakes of the past can help us avoid them in the future.

I often think about the lesson of the humble broom. For many years people earned their living making brooms one at a time, crafting them in their homes or in small workshops. Later, factories arose to employ large numbers of people, still making brooms by hand one at a time. This continued until the arrival of steam-powered equipment, like the stitching machines that enabled a single operator to mass-produce many brooms faster and cheaper. Bye bye, handmade brooms, because those craftsmen could not compete with the lower-cost brooms. Now who was responsible for the loss of employment of thousands of broom makers across the country? Was it the inventor of the steam devices? Or the capitalist companies that utilized the newer machinery to make the cheaper brooms? Or perhaps was it the consumers who purchased the cheaper brooms? Consumers ultimately determine who stays in business and who fails. It is the consumer who decides to purchase or not purchase the goods.

This is played out again and again in the exhibits of our museum. And it's still true today. Inventors and technology don't put people out of business. Neither do the companies or businesses in China or India. It is still the consumers who do so by buying goods for the lowest price. With new technology and more rapid means of communication and transportation, we are in a global economy. Ultimately most businesses and companies – and, of course, their workers – are competing against similar companies all over the world. The United States is no longer able to prosper by merely providing low-cost items. We must constantly develop new products and new processes to beat global competitors and provide meaningful jobs for our workers and their families. We still need brooms, but very few are handmade or made by steam-powered machinery, not in this age of computerized equipment and robotics.

It is management's responsibility to try to anticipate changes in technology, both in the manufacturing process and the development of new products to stay ahead of the competition from existing and new startup companies. If it fails, everyone loses, from investors to workers and suppliers and all of us who benefit from the taxes the company pays. Meanwhile, it is the workers' responsibility to wisely use the machinery and equipment developed by new technology, to learn to be more productive. The more effective workers are, the better the company can stay ahead of the competition. It's a partnership. If management fails to look ahead or if labor fails to adapt, both lose as does as everyone else effected by their missteps.

A walk through the museum and its many exhibits gives us many examples of the tragic consequences of management, labor and government's failure to adapt to new ideas and technology. Being reminded of these failures can inspire us to try harder to look ahead and plan more effectively.

One good idea does not last long and if the company is not constantly striving to improve and develop new and better ideas and products, a competitor surely will. The result can be disastrous to a local company. In the previous section, we also noted that, for example, one needs only to look at the major manufacturers in the Huntington area in the 1950s and ask where they are today. Houdaille Industries made some of the finest steel chrome-plated car bumpers available in the world. Did they go out of business because someone made a stronger or even a cheaper steel bumper? No. They went out of business because automobile manufacturers switched to plastic lightweight bumpers to improve gas consumption. Who missed this technological or societal change? Should anyone have seen it coming and tried to switch to plastic bumpers? Would the labor force been willing to make the necessary changes? Would the investors have been willing to abandon the substantial capital already invested in its old plant and put extensive additional monies into a new plant and equipment? We also cited the various glass bottling plants like Owens and Kerr glass, some of the finest bottle makers in the United States at the time. What happened to them? Same questions and unfortunately the same answers. Plastic. The list is quite long and the results almost always the same. Those that failed to adapt to change suffered the consequences and are no longer in business.

Which companies today, for the same reasons, will not be around in 50 years, or perhaps, even 10 or 20 years from now?

Every leader, owner and member of management constantly needs to be looking ahead, not resting on its laurels of past success. The clear message of the past is that someone else is quietly using newer technology or better ideas to try and put them out of business.

And it is not only business that needs to think this way. The same concerns should occupy parents, teachers and government leaders, all of us responsible for preparing today's young people for the world they will be living and working in. How dramatically different it will be from the world in which we grew up!

One example from the museum comes to mind. For hundreds of years, a skilled lathe operator with exceptional eye-hand coordination produced beautiful, useful items, both in wood and metal, on machines powered by various energy sources, progressing from a foot on a treadle to water to steam to electricity. Regardless of the advances in the machinery itself or the power sources, there was always a skilled operator required. One might assume that this would always be true. Surely there would always be good jobs for skilled lathe operators. However, in our technological world, a computerized robot now operates the lathes. The human jobs are to program and maintain the robots. In the new world, it is important to be able to design, build, program and maintain equipment and machinery, mostly computerized. The manual operations no longer require humans. To prepare today's students for jobs of the past is like teaching automobile mechanics on cars of the 1950s or training radio and TV repairmen to replace tubes instead of transistors and computer chips.

We must teach our students about a vastly different world they will occupy as well as how dramatically smaller the world is today, both as to travel and communication. Our children come into a world in which people in China, India and places all over the planet participate in a single global economy. This worldwide competition affects even our largest companies like General Motors and General Electric. Our students must become the brightest and best not just in West Virginia, Ohio and Kentucky or even just in the United States, but in the world. It is the greatest challenge faced by any generation. How can we – as parents, teachers, school administrators, elected officials and concerned citizens – help the children prepare for that future?

We believe one way is to experience the museum and discover that change and having to adapt to change is nothing new. Change is as old as our wonderful hills. Our Appalachian ancestors endured unbelievable change as they struggled to cross the mountains, build their own homes, raise their own food and even make their own clothes and footwear. How all of these things were done constantly changed as new and better ways were developed to do them. People were always striving to figure out how to do more, better, for less.

If our ancestors could successfully adapt, so can we. We just need to be willing to work as hard and never succumb to that old complaint that "we never did it that way before." Change is hard. We all have a tendency to want to preserve the status quo. Having thought a great deal about change, I myself have come to the conclusion that the only person who really *wants* a change is a wet baby. Mr. Darwin did not say it is the survival of the strongest or fastest or even the most intelligent -- it was the survival of the ones most likely to adapt.

Come to Heritage Farm with your family, students, coworkers and management. Come as church leaders or community leaders. We welcome all who are interested in learning more about our heritage and the fascinating people who persevered against unbelievable hardships to give us a quality of life we often take for granted today. We hope you will leave with a stronger sense of our responsibility to make sure future generations are prepared for the different world they will inherit.

ABOUT THE AUTHORS

Mike

A. Michael (Mike) Perry and his wife, Henriella Perry, are Co-Founders of Heritage Farm Museum and Village, which consists of more than twenty reconstructed log and other buildings dedicated to West Virginia's Appalachian Ancestors and educating others about their ingenuous and creative way of life. This has been a lifelong dream in the making and is the "retirement" project of the Perry's. He and his wife were awarded the Donald R. Myers Humanitarian award by the Appalachian Regional Commission in 2010.

Mr. Perry graduated from Marshall University in 1958 with a Bachelor of Arts Degree and was first in his class and Order of the Coif from the West Virginia University College of Law in 1961. He was given an Honorary Doctor of Humane Letters Degree from Marshall University in 1999 after serving as its Undefeated Interim President wherein MU had gone 15-0 in Football and were 10-0 in Basketball as his term ended. (About his Undefeated Presidency, Mike often remarks, "Might as well take credit for something good you had nothing to do with, because you certainly will be blamed for bad things that you had nothing to do with!").

Mike Perry has been a key leader in West Virginia's business, education and health communities throughout his successful career. As former Chairman and CEO of Key Centurion Bancshares, West Virginia's first billion dollar banking organization, he helped guide the organization through a number of transitions in its growth toward becoming Banc One West Virginia Corporation, as it later became Bank One, West Virginia, NA, which is now Chase Bank.

Before joining The First Huntington National Bank as its Chairman in 1981, he was a partner with the law firm of Huddleston, Bolen, Beatty, Porter and Copen in Huntington, West Virginia and served as State Chairman of the Young Lawyers Section of the West Virginia State Bar. In 1999, he was one of the charter members recognized by the West Virginia Bar Foundation Fellows Program.

He has served as Chairman of the West Virginia Chamber of Commerce, the West Virginia Bankers Association and the University System of West Virginia Board of Trustees and as Co-Chairman of West Virginia Celebration 2000. He has also taught adult Sunday School classes at what is now known as the New Baptist Church for over 35 years.

His leadership and commitment have earned him such honors as being named "Banker of the Decade" by the West Virginia Bankers Association and twice was named "Citizen of the Year" by the Huntington Herald Dispatch. Mike Perry is a "Charter Member" of the Business Hall of Fame for both Marshall University and West Virginia University. Today, he continues to enjoy collecting and constructing exhibits with family and friends at Heritage Farm.

Audy

Audy M. Perry, Jr. and his wife, Laura, coordinate the educational programming at Heritage Farm Museum and Village, assisting thousands of school children each year in learning more about the strong Appalachian past in order to inspire children to dream big for the future. Mr. Perry is also a partner with the law firm of Huddleston Bolen LLP in Huntington, West Virginia where he has been named a Rising Star by West Virginia Super Lawyers and was an inaugural inductee of the State Journal's Generation Next award.

Audy graduated summa cum laude from West Virginia Wesleyan College in 1993 with a Bachelor of Arts Degree and was Managing Editor of the West Virginia Law Review prior to graduating Order of the Coif from the West Virginia University College of Law in 1996.

Active in the local community and State, Audy is a Board member of the Huntington Regional Chamber of Commerce, Cabell Huntington Convention & Visitors Bureau, Foster Foundation, the West Virginia Law Institute and has taught teen Sunday School classes at what is now known as the New Baptist Church for over 15 years. One of Audy's favorite activities is sharing the petting zoo and wagon rides with friends and family at Heritage Farm.

HERITAGE FARM FOUNDATION
BY MIKE & AUDY PERRY

Industrious, ingenious, visionary, creative, entrepreneurial: these are not terms commonly used today to describe the people of Appalachia. Yet, they should be. Our cultural ancestors were all of these things and more. Those early settlers who crossed the mountains to tame the wilderness built the foundation for the industrial age and the American Century. They had the vision to look out from the settled east coast into the wilderness of the Appalachian Mountains and see opportunity. They had fortitude to make their vision reality. They had the ingenuity and creativity to hone a life out of tree and rock, and to build the towns and mines and railroads that we benefit from still today.

Our forefathers and mothers did not come over those mountains, carve out a hard-fought existence, and thrive among the challenges – all for their children to live simply waiting for someone else to fix their problems. Nor did they tirelessly work, at great personal cost and sacrifice, to provide the coal, timber, and steel that made this Nation's industrial revolution possible - only to find that their children fail to share in its created wealth. The social indicators we see every day, drug addiction, high dropout rates, obesity, and rampant depression, are all symptomatic of a people who are losing hope and their sense of purpose.

While we can appreciate the many social and economic factors that have contributed to our current dilemma, we must refuse to simply wait in a half-hearted wish for things to be better. We must take a firm hold of our future, dream big dreams, plan for success, and change our own course. To this end, Mike and Henriella Perry have created the Heritage Farm Foundation, a 501(c)(3) charitable organization which operates the Heritage Farm Museum & Village with the goal of providing a place where people of all walks of life can learn the story of Appalachia and realize what we, as individuals, families, communities, and companies can become.

The Foundation is currently seeking financial support to help build on the work Mike and Henriella began over 30 years ago and to help transform this remarkable center for Appalachian heritage into a destination where school children, families, businesses, and faith groups can learn about their rich heritage and understand that flowing within their veins are the same characteristics and abilities that their ancestors had, that the challenges they face are no more difficult than what their predecessors overcame, and that they are capable of building successful lives, strong families, and thriving businesses and communities, if they are willing to work as industriously and creatively as their ancestors.

Heritage Farm annually helps thousands of school children and families connect with the Appalachian Past and their Dreams for the Future. If you are interested in learning more about Heritage Farm and its mission, please contact us by email at hfmv@comcast.net, by phone at 304-522-1244; by U.S. Mail at 3300 Harvey Road, Huntington, WV 25704 or visit us online at www.heritagefarmmuseum.com. Heritage Farm is owned and operated by the Heritage Farm Foundation, a non-profit 501(c)(3) organization so any donations are tax deductible as allowed by law. Thank you for your interest in Heritage Farm. Together, we can learn from our strong past, appreciate the blessings of today, and work toward a brighter tomorrow.